The Dream of Europa

The Triumph of Peace

A Masque

First published by O-Books, 2015
O-Books is an imprint of John Hunt Publishing Ltd., Laurel House, Station Approach,
Alresford, Hants, SO24 9JH, UK
office1@jhpbooks.net
www.johnhuntpublishing.com

For distributor details and how to order please visit the 'Ordering' section on our website.

Text copyright: Nicholas Hagger 2015

ISBN: 978 1 78535 116 7
Library of Congress Control Number: 2015937442

A CIP catalogue record for this book is available from the British Library.

Design: Stuart Davies

Printed in the USA by Edwards Brothers Malloy

We operate a distinctive and ethical publishing philosophy in all areas of
our business, from our global network of authors to production and
worldwide distribution.

The Dream of Europa

The Triumph of Peace

A Masque

Nicholas Hagger

BOOKS

Winchester, UK
Washington, USA

Books published by Nicholas Hagger

The Fire and the Stones

Selected Poems

The Universe and the Light

A White Radiance

A Mystic Way

Awakening to the Light

A Spade Fresh with Mud

The Warlords

Overlord

A Smell of Leaves and Summer

The Tragedy of Prince Tudor

The One and the Many

Wheeling Bats and a Harvest Moon

The Warm Glow of the Monastery Courtyard

The Syndicate

The Secret History of the West

The Light of Civilization

Classical Odes

Overlord, one-volume edition

Collected Poems 1958–2005

Collected Verse Plays

Collected Stories

The Secret Founding of America

The Last Tourist in Iran

The Rise and Fall of Civilizations

The New Philosophy of Universalism

The Libyan Revolution

Armageddon

The World Government

The Secret American Dream

A New Philosophy of Literature

My Double Life 1: This Dark Wood

My Double Life 2: A Rainbow over the Hills

Selected Poems: Quest for the One

Selected Stories: Follies and Vices of the Modern Elizabethan Age

"'Masque', a form of amateur histrionic entertainment, originally consisting of dancing and acting in dumb show, the performers being masked, afterwards including dialogue and song, 1562; a dramatic composition for this kind of entertainment, 1605."

The Shorter Oxford English Dictionary

"'Masque', a dramatic and musical entertainment, especially of the 16th and 17th centuries, originally of pantomime, later with metrical dialogue; a dramatic composition for this."

The Concise Oxford Dictionary

To all Universalists, this masque that celebrates a unified Europe at peace.

The front cover shows Europa on a mosaic floor in a Roman villa found c.1900 in Trinquetaille, Arles, France, dating to end of 2nd century or beginning of 3rd century AD. Europa is seen against an enlarged Europe and surrounded by a circle of 50 stars representing the 28 member states of the EU and 22 states yet to join the EU.

"The man of letters as such, is not concerned with the political or economic map of Europe; but he should be very much concerned with its cultural map.... The man of letters... should be able to take a longer view than either the politician or the local patriot.... The cultural health of Europe, including the cultural health of its component parts, is incompatible with extreme forms of both nationalism and internationalism.... The responsibility of the man of letters at the present time... should be vigilantly watching the conduct of politicians and economists, for the purpose of criticizing and warning, when the decisions and actions of the politicians and economists are likely to have cultural consequences. Of these consequences the man of letters should qualify himself to judge. Of the possible cultural consequences of their activities, politicians and economists are usually oblivious; the man of letters is better qualified to foresee them, and to perceive their seriousness."

T.S. Eliot, *The Man of Letters and the Future of Europe*, 1944

CONTENTS

Dramatis Personae

Characters in order of appearance:

Zeus
Europa
50 representatives of 50 states –
    28 members of the EU:
        Germany
        Italy
        The UK
        Ireland
        France
        Belgium
        Netherlands
        Luxembourg
        Austria
        Slovenia
        Malta
        Portugal
        Spain
        Cyprus
        Croatia
        Estonia
        Latvia
        Lithuania
        Poland
        Hungary
        Czech Republic
        Slovakia
        Bulgaria
        Romania
        Greece
        Sweden
        Denmark
        Finland

22 yet to join the EU:
Turkey
Switzerland
Iceland
Norway
Liechtenstein
Monaco
Andorra
San Marino
Serbia
Albania
Kosovo
Bosnia and Herzegovina
Macedonia
Montenegro
Moldova
Ukraine
Azerbaijan
Georgia
Armenia
Russia
Belarus
Kazakhstan

9 Muses
9 Wise Men (or 9 shades):
Ficino
Augustus
Napoleon
Charlemagne
Kant
Justinian
Dante
Erasmus
Sir Thomas More

VIPs:
Jean Monnet

Winston Churchill
Robert Schuman
David Rockefeller
Paul-Henri Spaak
Nicole Fontaine
José Barroso
Giuliano Amato
Angela Merkel
Jean-Claude Juncker

Locations:

Berlin
Auschwitz
Metz
Zurich University
London
Festival Hall, Strasbourg
Salon d l'Horloge of the Quai d'Orsay, Paris
Hotel De Bilderberg, Oosterbeek
Grand Salon, Brussels
[Suez]
[Hungary]
Palazzo dei Conservatori on Capitoline Hill, Rome
Schengen, Luxembourg
Luxembourg
Berlin
Maastricht, Netherlands
Amsterdam
Nice
Rome
Brussels
Jerónimos Monastery, Lisbon
Lisbon
Berlaymont building, Brussels
Court of Justice, Luxembourg

Preface

Masques and Europe

The masque was a courtly entertainment performed in 16th and early-17th century Europe, including England. A masque was only played once, and celebrated an event at court. It often flattered the monarch, who often had a masked non-speaking part as did Henry VIII, James I and Charles I. It included music, dancing and singing, and the professional actors hired to speak and sing varied between eight and sixteen in number and wore elaborate costumes. On special occasions a band of masked players unexpectedly appeared at a nobleman's gates, performed at a social gathering in his Great Hall and danced with the guests. At the end of the entertainment they took off their masks and mingled with the audience, which in London comprised courtiers.

In England Ben Jonson's masques were performed in the Banqueting Hall of the Whitehall Palace during the Christmas holiday, often on Twelfth Night. (The Banqueting Hall preceded the Banqueting House, which was built between 1619 and 1622.) *The Masque of Blackness* was performed before the Stuart court in the Banqueting Hall on 6 January 1605. It was written at the request of Anne of Denmark, queen consort of James I. The masquers were disguised as Africans and their blackness was supposed to be cured by James I. This was impossible to show, and after Jonson's *Hymenaei*, or *The Masque of Hymen*, which was written for the Earl of Essex's wedding before a Roman altar on 15 January 1606, there was a sequel, *The Masque of Beauty*, which was also performed in the Banqueting Hall, on 10 January 1608. *The Masque of Queens* was performed on 2 February 1609 and contained an antimasque, unlike the previous masques.

Jonson's *Oberon, The Fairy Prince* was performed in the Banqueting Hall on 1 January 1611. The front curtains displayed a map of the British Isles, and the fairy prince Oberon (based on James I) arrived to bestow order and rule benevolently. Nymphs and satyrs danced joyfully. *Christmas, His Masque* was performed at the court during Christmas 1616, when Christmas entered with his attendants. *The*

Masque of Augurs was performed on 6 January 1622. It praised the arranged marriage between Prince Charles (the future Charles I) and the Spanish Infanta, and Prince Charles himself led the dance of the masquers. The masque included some thoroughly-researched Roman augury.

Shakespeare's masque scenes in *The Tempest* were influenced by Jonson, and there had also been masque scenes in *Romeo and Juliet* and *Henry VIII*. Spenser's *Faerie Queene* (book 1, canto 4) contains a processional masque of The Seven Deadly Sins. John Milton wrote *A Masque Presented at Ludlow Castle, 1634 (Comus)*. Such dramatic masques ended in 1640 with *Salmacida Spolia*. Masques were dependent on the court, and the fall of the monarchy and consequent collapse of the court brought them to an end. The Puritans closed the theatres in 1642, and in the 1660s when they reopened the masque turned into opera. The poet John Dryden and the composer Henry Purcell collaborated on productions that were part-masque and part-opera. Thomas Arne wrote a masque, *Alfred* (1740), which included the first performance of 'Rule Britannia'. Shelley wrote *The Masque of Anarchy* about the Peterloo Massacre of 1819. Several musicians wrote masques, including Ralph Vaughan Williams, who wrote *Job: A Masque for Dancing*. Also in the 20th century William Empson wrote a masque, *The Birth of Steel*, in honour of the Queen's visit to Sheffield on 27 October 1954. Its relatively undramatic verse only took 15 minutes to perform. In the course of the masque Queen Elizabeth II was addressed as a "goddess" in keeping with the masque's tradition of flattering the patron. (The Queen returned the compliment by bestowing a knighthood on Empson in 1979.)

The origins of the masque are in doubt. In England Richard II took part in "mumming" (masked mime) as early as 1377. In Italy the masquerade was a carnival entertainment akin to "mumming". In France the performance became more of a spectacle. Throughout Europe there were "guisings" or "disguisings" in which a masked allegorical figure addressed a courtly audience. In England the masque's immediate forerunner was the dumbshow of the kind found in Thomas Kyd's *The Spanish Tragedy* (first performed 1587) and in Shakespeare's *A Midsummer Night's Dream* (1595–1596, the wedding of

Pyramus and Thisbe), *Hamlet* (1600–1602) and *Pericles, Prince of Tyre* (1607–1608). Masques performed for Elizabeth I emphasised the unity of her kingdom and the peace and concord that flourished in her realm.

Formally, the masque had five parts: the prologue or poetic induction; the antimasque (a spectacle of disorder and chaos) which preceded the masque; the masque (which transformed the disorder into order and harmony, and provided a resolution); the revels (which rejoiced at the resolution and broke down the barrier between stage and spectator); and the epilogue.

This masque, *The Dream of Europa*, is about the birth of a unified Europe. The representatives of 50 European states are on stage throughout the playing time. In the prologue, Zeus entrusts Europa (the goddess of Europe) with the task of bringing peace to a Europe ravaged by the Second World War. In the antimasque, Europeans chant their misery and wretchedness at the disorder and chaos in Europe, aided by film on a large screen. In the masque, Europa turns the disorder into order and brings the resolution of a unified state that begins with the implementation of the Treaty of Lisbon. In the revels, Europeans rejoice at the new unified Europe and celebrate. And in the epilogue, Europa hands the European Union back to Zeus on course to become a United States of Europe and to have 50 states like the United States of America. His problem solved, Zeus looks ahead to a World State.

The Dream of Europa, which is subtitled *The Triumph of Peace*, contrasts the disorder of Europe in 1945 with the order in Europe 70 years later in 2015, and by rooting the Treaty of Lisbon in the ruins of Berlin I am reminding the audience of why a unified Europe has been created and of the peace that has been achieved.

However, despite the order that has been established there are still discordant voices – from Greece, Italy, Spain and the UK – and the revels are interrupted by disputes within Europe that still have to be resolved. Not all Europeans were pleased that the European Community passed into a more unitary European Union as a result of the Maastricht Treaty of 1993, and Eurosceptics now regard the European Union and its eurozone as a failed experiment.

There is evidence that Russia wants to recover the Baltic states, which it still regards as being within the Russian sphere of influence, and keeping Europe together will prevent Russian expansion whereas fragmenting Europe with exits (by Greece and the UK) would open the way for Russian expansion. *The Dream of Europa* calls for European unity at a time when the unity of Europe is threatened.

Towards the end of the revels, Churchill (my MP during the war) lambasts the UK representative for having forgotten the war and for putting domestic concerns such as immigration and the abuse of the benefit system above its vision of unity. He reminds her of the chaos in 1945 and the triumph of peace in 2014. It is my hope that the UK will come to share Churchill's perspective.

Europe has done extremely well during the last 70 years. It is a Union of 28 states, and as can be seen from the diagram on p.xviii the remaining 22 of the 50 European states are members of one or more of the 17 supranational bodies that form groupings of European nation-states. The dream of Europa is that one day the EU will consist of 50 European states, a step towards a Universalist World State. My work, *My Double Life 2: A Rainbow over the Hills*, was subtitled *The Vision of Unity*, and the vision of unity is what is now needed to create a United States of Europe that can lead all the continents of the earth into a coming World State. Such a State can abolish war, famine, disease and poverty by international law and greatly benefit humankind.

I had the idea for *The Dream of Europa* in April 2010, and I was in touch with the European Agency for Fundamental Rights. The project was shelved in May 2010 due to the euro crisis involving Greece (a problem still with us in 2015), and the idea was pushed to one side until late 2014, when the European debate intensified in the UK. As a man of letters I am pleased to be able to add this masque to the other *genres* in which I have worked, which include lyric poems, classical odes, epic poems, verse plays and short stories. The masque has always been a court entertainment, and it is my hope that there will be a production of this work in Brussels to mark an anniversary attended by European leaders.

19–20 January 2015

Groupings of Nation-States and Positioning of Representatives

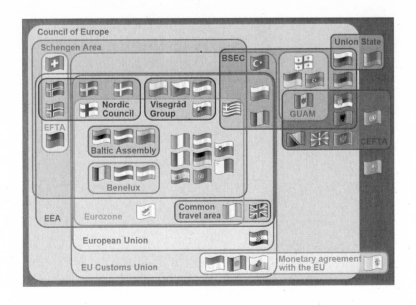

Groupings of 50 European nation-states (and Vatican City) in 17
supranational bodies
(For identification of flags, see pp.88–93)

Switzerland									Turkey		Georgia		Russia	Belarus
Iceland	Sweden	Denmark	Poland	Czech Republic	Hungary		Bulgaria	Ukraine	Azerbaijan				Armenia	
Norway	Finland			Slovakia	Greece		Romania		Moldova		Serbia			
Liechtenstein	Estonia	Latvia	Lithuania	Italy	Austria	Slovenia		Bosnia and Herzegovina	Macedonia	Albania	Montenegro			Kosovo
	Belgium	Netherlands	Luxembourg	France	Germany	Malta								
				Spain	Portugal						Kazakhstan			
			Cyprus			Ireland	UK							
							Croatia							
					Monaco	Andorra	San Marino							
														Vatican City

Key to supranational bodies: groupings of nation-states and positioning of the 50 representatives (and Vatican City)

THE DREAM OF EUROPA

Prologue

(Berlin towards the end of the Second World War. 50 representatives of European nations stand in formation (see diagram and key on pp.xviii–xix). Their nationalities are identifiable from their dress and flags, and they will be listed on a programme note. At different times representatives step forward to speak lines or to embody a chorus. Before them stand the aged ZEUS and EUROPA. Film on a screen behind them of Berlin in ruins.)

Zeus:

It looks like an earthquake – Berlin, Europe:
Everywhere rubble of collapsed buildings
As if the earth had heaved. Humans did this,
Not Nature, dropping bombs on neighbouring
    states.
I want a peaceful and unified world,
Order and harmony. As the top god
I am frustrated that blundering man
Has undermined my efforts to bring in
A democratic World State with the power
To abolish war, famine and disease.
I gave my backing to first Hitler, then
To Stalin, but both disappointed me.
Fascism, Communism killed millions
And imposed tyrannies on humankind,
But they also imposed a levelling-down.
Traditions are right for a new Europe
That can incorporate its nation-states
And grow into a massive superstate
And bring peace and prosperity to close
On a billion Europeans. The first
Step is to create a common market
From which political union can grow.

As I'm disillusioned with world leaders,
Who're self-interested and can't be trusted,
I've chosen my protégée Europa,
To whom I've been a mentor and whose mind
I have 'impregnated' with one-world seed,
To gestate and bear an infant World State:
A European Union that can grow
Into a United States of Europe
So Europe, Asia and the Americas
Can one day unite in a one-world State.
My dear Europa, you have always held
A special place in my heart and my hopes.
You know I want a unified mankind,
All humankind equal under world law.
Are you now ready to begin the task
That weighs so heavily upon my mind,
To bring order to this chaos of war
And establish a resurging Europe
In which all citizens can live at peace,
A paradise, a forerunner of states
That can combine in a peaceful union
And be an example to humankind?

Europa: I am, and I am honoured that you've placed
Your trust in me. I will happily share
The burden of shouldering the dark world
Which, stooping like Atlas, you have endured.
I will gladly assist you in quelling
Europe and replacing its disorder
And cruel war with order and smiling peace.
I accept the responsibility.

Zeus: Well spoken. You'll be like a Minister,
Autonomous but reporting to me.
I'm your President and Prime Minister,
And so a word of advice at the start.

I want a democratic World State, not
A tyranny, the self-interested
Élite's New World Order run to enrich
Themselves and ignoring poor humankind.
You may have to ally with this *élite*
To bring to birth your free common market,
But when it's served its purpose you must dump
All who'd loot Europe's assets for themselves,
Twine them round your finger, and when they've
    done
The work you want, sever the connection.
You must be ruthless in the cause of peace.

Europa: I will do as you say for I'm loyal
To your vision of a united earth.
I have a dream of the most dignified,
Free, equal, rightful, just, utopian
Society that ever existed.

Antimasque

(Auschwitz. Film of Auschwitz, smoking chimneys, Nazi executions, torture, enslavements and discrimination against Jews and other minorities. Sombre music evoking Europe's ruin. The 50 representatives mime and dance from their standing positions, aghast at the horrors, averting their eyes, not wanting to look at the screen. Then all 50 become a CHORUS and chant. Sections of the 50 can chant different lines in a kind of contrapuntal dialogue.)

Chorus:

Alas, we lament our ruined Europe.
Alas, we lament the miserable
Conditions ordinary people endure.
We are devastated by mass slaughter.
Our ruined homes, amid mounds of rubble,
Bombs blasting round us, demolishing all,
No shops for food, no water, no shelter.
We have been squatting among dead bodies,
The stench of death has filled us with disgust.
We are listless, we feel a lassitude,
We're hungry from eating scraps of stale bread.
We all feel sick, we have no energy.

(The representatives each indicate their war suffering in two lines, to film and sombre music. As EACH OF THE 50 chants, a snippet of film on the screen shows the war misery in that representative's country.)

Germany:

Hitler rubbled Berlin's streets and slaughtered
Three hundred and fifty thousand Germans.

Italy:

Mussolini marched us into defeats
In Greece, in Russia and North Africa.

UK:
The UK stood alone, *Blitz*ed but unbowed.
Ruined London liberated Europe.

Ireland:
Ireland was neutral but gave the Allies
News of Atlantic storms before D-Day.

France:
France was wretched under occupation
And dreamt of victory for the Resistance.

Belgium:
Belgium was invaded by the *Blitzkrieg*
And occupied by the murderous Nazis.

Netherlands:
The Dutch were overrun in just five days,
Nazi occupation lasted five years.

Luxembourg:
Luxembourg was annexed by the Nazis
And became a 'province' of the Third Reich.

Austria:
Austria lost independence when we were
Incorporated into the Third Reich.

Slovenia:
Slovenia was divided, partisans
Drove out the Italians and the Nazis.

Malta:
Malta was close to Axis shipping lanes
And was bombed during the siege of Malta.

Portugal:
Portugal's right-wing dictatorship kept
Us neutral during the Second World War.

Spain:
Spain was neutral under military
Dictatorship and steered clear of the war.

Cyprus:
Cyprus fought in the British Army in
Both wars, hoping for union with Greece.

Croatia: The Axis occupied Croatia and
Killed three hundred and thirty thousand Serbs.

Estonia: Estonia was occupied by Soviets,
Then by the Germans, then the Red Army.

Latvia: Latvia was occupied by Soviets
And the Nazis, who killed all Latvian Jews.

Lithuania: Lithuania also, and two hundred
Thousand Lithuanian Jews were murdered.

Poland: The Nazis occupied Poland and killed
Five million – gassed three million Polish Jews.

Hungary: The Nazis occupied Hungary and sent
Four hundred thousand Jews to Auschwitz.

Czech Republic: Czech territory was occupied and three
Hundred and fifty thousand Czechs were killed.

Slovakia: Slovakia became a German puppet
Regime till liberated by Russia.

Bulgaria: Bulgaria was forced to join the Axis
And was invaded by the Soviets.

Romania: Romania supplied Germany with oil
And was bombed by the Allies, then changed
sides.

Greece: Greece was occupied by Germans, thousands
Died in combat or camps, or starved to death.

Sweden: Sweden was cut off by Nazi blockades
And spent the war under German influence.

Denmark:

Denmark fell to the Germans in two hours
And the occupation brought misery.

Finland:

Finland fought the Soviet Union twice
And then forced the Germans out of the north.

Turkey:

Turkey remained neutral but declared war
On Germany and Japan at the end.

Switzerland:

Switzerland remained neutral and traded
With both sides and amassed gold in its banks.

Iceland:

Iceland was occupied by the British,
Then the Americans, and missed the war.

Norway:

Norway was occupied by the Nazis,
At least thirty thousand were imprisoned.

Liechtenstein:

Liechtenstein stayed neutral, but Czechs and Poles
Expropriated all our 'German' lands.

Monaco:

Italy, then Germany occupied
The principality of Monaco.

Andorra:

Andorra remained neutral and became
A route for getting airmen out of France.

San Marino:

The British bombed San Marino, thinking
It had been overrun by the Germans.

Serbia:

The Axis powers killed Serbians in camps,
Three hundred and forty thousand were killed.

Albania:

Albania, occupied by Italy,
Then Germany, endured a wretched time.

Kosovo: The Axis assigned most of Kosovo
To Italian-controlled Albania.

Bosnia and
Herzegovina: Bosnia was ceded to Croatia, Jews
And Serbs were genocided in eight camps.

Macedonia: Macedonia groaned under pro-Axis
Albania and German Bulgaria.

Montenegro: Italy, then Germany occupied
Montenegro and spread great misery.

Moldova: In Moldova, a Soviet republic,
Two hundred thousand died of starvation.

Ukraine: Eight million starved to death in the famine
In Ukraine, then Germany colonised.

Azerbaijan: Azerbaijan was Soviet and supplied
Oil and gas and fought in the Red Army.

Georgia: Georgia was Soviet and its oilfields were
Out of reach of the thrusting Axis powers.

Armenia: Armenia was Soviet and sent hundreds
Of thousands of its troops to the front line.

Russia: Russia repelled a German invasion
But endured twenty-seven million deaths.

Belarus: Germans occupied Soviet Belarus
And razed over two-thirds of our cities.

Kazakhstan: Kazakhstan stayed out of the Axis reach
And rehoused Russians and their industries.

All in chorus:

Alas, our misery and our torment.
Save us from executions and torture,
From slavery and compulsory labour.
Our souls are tired from five long years of war,
And now swathes of East Europe are falling
Under Soviet control, and as fast as
One despotism ends a new one starts.
Alas, will no one help? Who will save us
From the wretched lives we've all had to bear?
We dream of democratic states that reach
The borders of Russia, but have no hope.
All's disorder, confusion and chaos.

(EUROPA *turns to the Nine Muses, who are standing
to one side on the left of the stage.*)

Europa:

Nine Muses, I need you to inspire me
To save these people from their wretched lives.
Calliope, with your writing tablet
Inspire me with an epic Union.
I need the sweep of your epic vision.
Clio, with your scrolls teach me history
So I may draw nations into Union.
Erato, with your *cithara* or lyre
Inspire me with your lyric poetry
So I may turn their plaintive woe to joy.
Euterpe, with your *aulos*, your old flute,
Inspire me with your music so I may
Turn wretchedness into prosperity.
Melpomene, with your tragic mask please
Inspire me with your tragedy so I
May turn this tragic scene into beauty.
Polyhymnia, pensive beneath your veil,
Inspire me with your sacred poetry
So our choruses guide us to Union.
Terpsichore, who carries a lyre, please

12

Inspire me with your dancing so dancers
May dance the joy of creating Union.
Thalia, with your comic mask please inspire
This masque so I may satirise all who
Would stand in the way of Europe's Union,
So I may ridicule their warped follies.
And Urania, with your celestial globe
And pair of compasses please inspire me
So with your astronomy I may read
The stars and predict our Union's growth
Accurately, and our State's expansion.
And now, Nine Muses, conjure by your art,
Assisted by mighty Zeus, Lord of all,
Nine Wise Men who dwell in the Elysian Fields
To come up through Hades and advise me.

(*The* NINE MUSES *come to the front centre of the
stage and raise their arms and conjure. They chant.*)

Nine Muses: Shades of the glorious dead, we conjure you,
Step forth from the eternal sunshine round
The banks of the river Oceanus,
That happy place in the Isles of the Blessed
In the western ocean at the earth's end.
Traverse the darkness round the earth and cross
Through Hades and return to this daylight,
You shades of men who still have much to give.
Step forth, I command you, two Emperors,
Augustus and Charlemagne; law-maker
Justinian; visionary Dante;
Sir Thomas More who wrote *Utopia*;
Erasmus; conqueror Napoleon;
Uniter Ficino; philosopher Kant.
Nine spirits who can dream a new Europe.

(One by one the shades gather on stage as they are summoned. Each is clad in a black cloak. EUROPA speaks.)

Europa:

Spirits, I command you in Zeus's name
To spend time at my side and inform me,
For I must now live in complexity
And take into my soul all arguments
That represent every conflicting view
And quarrel with myself so a Union
Can be born from your range of opinions,
All opposites from east and west and all
Principles and democratic values,
That I may leave no idea untried as
I deliberate on the way forward.

(EUROPA addresses each of the nine Wise Men, and after they are spoken to each nods.)

Ficino, please advise on dignity,
On the dignity of citizens, as
You wrote of the dignity of the soul.
Augustus, champion of freedom, *vindex*
Libertatis in *Res Gestae*, advise
On the freedoms citizens should enjoy.
Napoleon, please advise on citizens'
Equality as your Code established
The equality of all before law.
Charlemagne, who based high army morale
On tribal solidarity, advise
On the citizens' solidarity.
Kant, please advise me on citizens' rights
As you wrote your *Doctrine of Rights*, and bring
Your purposive view of history to me.
And Justinian, please advise on justice
As you pushed through the *Codex Justinianus*.

Dante, who in *Convivio* appealed
For a universal monarch to rule,
Bring your vision of human unity.
Erasmus, the "Prince of the Humanists",
Who wrote *In Praise of Folly* staying with More,
Bring your wide knowledge of the human heart.
And Thomas More, bring your utopian
Idealism to imperfect Europe,
Help me build a perfect society.
And please draw near my living VIPs:
Jean Monnet, Robert Schuman and Winston
Churchill, who can all give me sound advice
As I begin to found institutions.
Please remain with me after you have died.

(*The* THREE VIPs *gather on the right of the stage, the opposite side from the nine shades' side. When they have died, they will put on black cloaks similar to those worn by the nine shades, and cross to join the shades on the left of the stage. The Nine Muses play their lyres and flute, and sway in dance. The* NINE SHADES *speak.*)

The nine shades: We will gladly share all our commonsense
As we advise on this growing Europe.
We're glad to be back among the living
And to strive once again to achieve goals,
A function we have missed in Hades' realm.

The three VIPs: We're glad to join this advisory body.

Masque

*(Lights dim and then brighten. 4 December 1945.
EUROPA turns to JEAN MONNET. Film of Monnet
on screen.)*

Europa: Jean Monnet, what is your plan for Europe?

Monnet: The Monnet Plan, which I have submitted
To General de Gaulle, who is our head,
To modernise the French economy,
For France to mine German coal in the Saar
And integrate the two economies
Under a common High Authority,
To weaken Germany and raise up France,
Remove the Saar to a Protectorate.
I am a humble French civil servant,
I hold no office but I have a Plan.

*(Lights dim and then brighten. 14 July 1946. Metz.
WINSTON CHURCHILL stands next to Robert
Schuman. Film of Churchill on screen.)*

Europa: Winston Churchill, you have seen the future.

Churchill: Franco-German reconciliation
In a united Europe – that's our path.

*(Lights dim and then brighten. 19 September 1946.
CHURCHILL speaks at Zurich University. Film of
Churchill speaking.)*

Churchill: I wish to speak to you today about
The tragedy of Europe. We must build
A kind of United States of Europe.

We must re-create the European
Family in a regional structure called
The United States of Europe. The first
Step is to form a Council of Europe.

(*Lights dim and then brighten. 1 January 1948. The*
REPRESENTATIVES OF BELGIUM, NETHER-
LANDS AND LUXEMBOURG *step forward. They*
chant. Film on screen.)

Belgium,
Netherlands and
Luxembourg: Even while war ravaged our continent
We signed the London Customs Convention,
A treaty to set up the Benelux
Customs Union and unify three states.

(*Lights dim and then brighten. 17 March 1948. Film on*
screen of the Treaty of Brussels being signed by the UK,
the Benelux three and France. EUROPA speaks.)

Europa: Belgium, France, Luxembourg, the Netherlands
And the UK have signed an expansion
Of last year's Anglo-French Dunkirk Treaty:
The Treaty of Brussels' mutual defence.

(*Lights dim and then brighten. 5 May 1949. London.*
Film of the Treaty of London establishing the Council of
Europe. Ten states sign: Belgium, Denmark, France,
Ireland, Italy, Luxembourg, Netherlands, Norway,
Sweden and the UK. EUROPA speaks.)

Europa: Ten states have implemented Churchill's call
For a body that shares democratic
And legal principles that are based on
Protecting human rights and our freedoms:

18

Belgium, Denmark, France, Ireland, Italy,
Luxembourg, Netherlands, Norway, Sweden
And Churchill's own redoubtable UK.
The Berlin blockade has set the western
Democratic *bloc* against the eastern
Communists, and west Germany against
East Germany, what is about to be
The Federal Republic of Germany
Against the Red German Democratic
Republic. Europe is completely split.

(EUROPA *turns to Robert Schuman, French Minister
of Foreign Affairs.*)

Robert Schuman, tell us what you have seen.

(*Lights dim and then brighten. 16 May 1949.
SCHUMAN speaks in the Festival Hall, Strasbourg.
Film on screen.*)

Schuman: We're carrying out a great experiment,
Fulfilment of the same recurrent dream
That for ten centuries has revisited
The peoples of Europe: their creation
Of an organisation that will end
War and guarantee an eternal peace.
The Roman Church and German *Führertum*
(Domination by dictatorship) failed
To create such a system. Audacious
Seers such as Dante, Erasmus, Abbé
De Saint-Pierre, Rousseau, Kant and Proudhon
   tried.
More's *Utopia* was found impractical.

(*More reacts indignantly from the group of VIPs.*)

The European spirit's proud to serve
A cultural family, a community,
And shuns hegemony and the selfish
Exploitation of others. Our century
Has witnessed clashes of nationalism
And seeks to reconcile the nation-states
In a supranational association
That safeguards each nation's diversities
And aspirations, and co-ordinates
Them like the regions within a nation.

*(Lights dim and then brighten. 23 September 1949.
SCHUMAN speaks at the fourth session of the United
Nations General Assembly. Film on screen.)*

Schuman: Our hope's that Germany will find its place
In the community of free nations,
In that European Community
Heralded by the Council of Europe.

*(Lights dim and then brighten. 9 May 1950. Film on
screen shows The Schuman Declaration delivered by the
French Minister of Foreign Affairs, Robert Schuman, in
the Salon de l'Horloge of the Quai d'Orsay in Paris.
Film on screen. MONNET and SCHUMAN.)*

Monnet: I've edited Schuman's declaration.
I'm a humble civil servant and hold
No office but I've shaped a key speech by
The French Minister of Foreign Affairs.

Schuman: France agrees to share and grow sovereignty
In a supranational Community,
To place all Franco-German coal and steel
Under a common High Authority
Within an organisation open

To all the other countries of Europe –
Regional integration that will make
War unthinkable and materially
Impossible: a new common market
For coal and steel. There should be a treaty.
The Schuman Declaration states the aims
Of the new European Coal and Steel
Community. They are: to mark the birth
Of a united Europe and make war
Between its member states impossible;
To encourage world peace and unify
Europe democratically, step by step,
As the world's first supranational body;
To create a common market across
The Community and revitalise
The European and world economies.

(*Lights dim and then brighten. 18 April 1951. Film on screen shows the signing of the Treaty of Paris in the Salon de l'Horloge, Clock Room, of the Quai d'Orsay in Paris. The* REPRESENTATIVES OF SIX NATIONS – *Belgium, Netherlands, Luxembourg, France, West Germany and Italy – step forward as do* MONNET *and* SCHUMAN *from the VIPs. They chant to film showing the European Coal and Steel Community.*)

Chorus of six
nations, Monnet
and Schuman: The Treaty of Paris: we have brought in
The ECSC, the European
Coal and Steel Community that will now
Neutralise competition in the Ruhr,
Prevent war between France and Germany.
Monnet, its architect, 's our President.
A continuation of Monnet's plan.
We call ourselves 'the supranational six'.

(The Nine Muses raise their arms and beam power into Europa. They beam power to Europa whenever there is a difficulty. EUROPA holds her hands above the heads of the six, Monnet and Schuman.)

Europa: Coal and steel's a first step, out of them can
You create a Common Market with full
Economic integration for six?

(Lights dim and then brighten. 3 September 1953. Film on screen of the European Convention on Human Rights coming into force, a brief and simple ceremony in the office of Anthony Lincoln, Acting Secretary-General of the Council of Europe. Jean-Pierre Kremer of Luxembourg has given a brief address before the issuing of a press release. EUROPA speaks.)

Europa: A great day for the Council of Europe
Has introduced an international
Treaty to protect human rights and our
Fundamental freedoms: The European
Convention on Human Rights, which will be
Protected in the European Court
Of Human Rights. The fourteen member states
Are committed to guaranteeing free
Elections, ending the death penalty
And preserving for all the rule of law.

(Lights dim and then brighten. 14 REPRESENTA-TIVES step forward: the representatives of Belgium, Denmark, France, Ireland, Italy, Luxembourg, Netherlands, Norway, Sweden, UK, Greece, Turkey, Iceland and Germany. All chant.)

14 representatives: We fourteen Council of Europe's early
Member states drew up The European

Convention on Human Rights, which looks back
To the English and American Bills
Of Rights and to the French Declaration
Of the Rights of Man and to the first part
Of the German Basic Law, and which states
Principles that courts have to interpret.
Its articles enshrine civil freedoms.

(*Lights dim and then brighten. The* 14 REPRESENTA-
TIVES *each chant one of articles 1–14 of Section I of
the European Convention on Human Rights. See
Appendix 2. Each article appears in film on screen.*)

Belgium: Our rights bind within our jurisdiction.

Denmark: All have a right to his or her own life.

France: All torture is prohibited –

Ireland: As is
Slavery, servitude and forced labour.

Italy: Everyone has the right to liberty.

Luxembourg: Everyone has the right to a fair trial.

Netherlands: No act that's not a crime can be punished.

Norway: Everyone has a right to privacy.

Sweden: And to free thought, conscience and religion.

UK: And a right to freedom of expression,

Greece: Free assembly and association,

Turkey: To marriage.

Iceland: And effective remedy
                   If authorities violate these rights.

Germany: Discrimination is prohibited.

All: And fifteen protocols, if signed by states,
                   Amend the framework of the Convention
                   Or expand the rights to be protected.

                   (*Lights dim and then brighten. 29 May 1954. Hotel De
                   Bilderberg, Oosterbeek.* DAVID ROCKEFELLER *enters
                   and speaks from shadows.*)

Rockefeller: I am responsible for this conference.
                   I have a vision, seek to counteract
                   Growing anti-Americanism
                   By holding a conference to promote
                   Atlanticism, co-operation
                   Between the US and Western Europe
                   In political and economic
                   Matters and in defence, and thereafter
                   An annual international conference.
                   I have another, more covert vision.
                   In common with Jean Monnet and Schuman
                   I've a vision of a common market
                   Within a unified Europe. I'm here
                   At Oosterbeek's Hotel De Bilderberg
                   But in the shadows, don't want the limelight.
                   On my behalf Józef Retinger has
                   Approached Prince Bernhard of the Netherlands,
                   Who then contacted Walter Bedell Smith,
                   Head of the CIA, and President
                   Eisenhower's adviser Jackson listed
                   Fifty delegates from eleven countries,

Two attendees from each nation who hold
Conservative and liberal points of view.
Eleven Americans are present.
My business interests coincide with this
Idea of a coming Common Market
And stepping-stone to a New World Order.

(*Rockefeller steps back into the shadows.*)

(*Lights dim and then brighten. 23 October 1954. The
Paris Conference in which the participating powers
including Belgium, Canada, Denmark, France, Greece,
Iceland, Italy, Luxembourg, Netherlands, Norway,
Portugal, Turkey, the UK and the US have reached
agreement on West Germany. The representative of
West Germany steps forward and is addressed by
EUROPA. Film on screen of the Paris Conference of
1954.*)

Europa: At conferences in London and Paris
We have agreed West Germany should have
Full sovereignty with NATO membership.
Occupation must end. West Germany
Can join the Brussels Treaty, which will now
Provide mutual defence for six nations:
Benelux, France, Italy, West Germany.

(*Lights dim and then brighten. 5 May 1955. JEAN
MONNET steps forward. Film on screen of Monnet's
resignation.*)

Monnet: The French have rejected a European
Defence Community, and I've resigned
From the High Authority in protest
And am working on nuclear energy –

(Europa holds her hands above Monnet's head. The VIPs approach and EUROPA refers in whispers.)

Europa: This will be known as the European
Atomic Energy Community.

(Lights dim and then brighten. 26 June 1956. Grand Salon, Belgian Foreign Ministry, Brussels. The first day of the Intergovernmental Conference on the Common Market and Euratom, headed by Paul-Henri Spaak, for delegates from the six nations of the European Coal and Steel Community: ECSC. Spaak refers to his Report on the General Common Market. This was written for the Intergovernmental Committee set up by the Foreign Ministers of the six member states of the ECSC following the Messina Conference in Brussels. The Committee met from 9 July 1955 to 20 April 1956, and the Report was presented on 21 April 1956. Film on screen of Spaak holding his Report and of the Conference. The chorus of 50 react favourably. PAUL-HENRI SPAAK enters and joins the VIPs.)

Europa: Paul-Henri Spaak, tell us what you have seen.

Spaak: As Chairman of the Spaak Committee, I
See my Report on a coming Common
European Market as the cornerstone
Of the Intergovernmental Conference
On the Common Market and Euratom
Which we are starting in the Grand Salon
Of the Belgian Foreign Ministry, Brussels.
Negotiations will continue in
Le château de Val Duchesse, Auderghem.

(Lights dim and then brighten. Film on screen of the Anglo-French-Israeli invasion of Suez on 1 November

*1956 and the Soviet invasion of Hungary on 4
November 1956. Film on screen shows
Intergovernmental Conference at le château de Val
Duchesse.)*

*(25 March 1957. Film on screen of the signing of the
Treaty of Rome at the Palazzo dei Conservatori on
Capitoline Hill, Rome.* SPAAK *steps forward.)*

Spaak: The outcome of this Conference is clear.
            The Treaty of Rome can now establish –
            Found – the European Economic
            Community in which the six reduce
            Customs duties progressively until
            There is a common customs union,
            A common market of goods, services,
            Workers and capital within the six.
            There will be common agricultural
            And transport policies, and social fund.
            All the communities – the EEC,
            Euratom and ECSC will share
            Both the Common Assembly and The Court
            Of Justice but the new communities –
            The EEC and Euratom – will have
            Their own Commissions and won't share the High
            Authority of the ECSC.

            *(*EUROPA *turns and speaks secretively, almost in a
            whisper, to David Rockefeller, who is lurking in the
            shadows.)*

Europa: These new communities could not exist
            But for the discussions that began at
            The Bilderberg Hotel in Oosterbeek
            At the invitation of Prince Bernhard.
            I want to thank you as the architect,

And co-founder with Józef Retinger,
Of that new Group, David Rockefeller,
In conjunction with the banking Rothschilds.
Though in the shadows, you shaped this Treaty.

(DAVID ROCKEFELLER *steps from the shadows.*)

Rockefeller   (*quietly*): My business interests are identical
With those of the EU. I want to see
The nation-states of Europe cast aside
Their sovereignty and work for common good
Within an expanding New World Order.

Europa   (*aside*): I am suspicious of this new order.
He did my bidding, helped the Treaty through
Behind the scenes, lobbying attendees.
But I am wary for is he being
Self-serving in supporting this Treaty?
Does he see profits in this new market?
(*Aloud.*) You've done well to persuade politicians
Of the six to join this Common Market.

(*David Rockefeller steps back into the shadows. The*
REPRESENTATIVES OF THE SIX *nations step*
forward.)

Chorus of the six,
Monnet,
Schuman and
Spaak: We rejoice that we now have a market
That integrates six of us, now the rest.

(*All* 50 REPRESENTATIVES *step forward and chant.*)

Chorus of 50:   We have lifted Europe from its ruins.
Again Europe is a good place to live.

Thank all you who signed the Treaty of Rome.
We can see Europe blossoming again.

(Lights dim and then brighten. 8 April 1965. Churchill and Schuman have put on black cloaks and have joined the shades on the left of the stage. Spaak has left the stage and stands in the shadows. Film on screen shows the six signing the Merger Treaty which will come into force on 1 July 1967. The REPRESENTATIVES OF THE SIX *step forward and chant.)*

The six:　　　　But now the Merger Treaty gladdens us,
　　　　　　　The Treaty of Brussels that looks ahead
　　　　　　　And brings common institutions to three
　　　　　　　Communities – EEC, Euratom
　　　　　　　And the ECSC – which are still known
　　　　　　　As the European Communities.
　　　　　　　The EEC's Commission and Council
　　　　　　　Replace Euratom's and ECSC's
　　　　　　　High Authority and Council, convert
　　　　　　　Them to one institutional structure,
　　　　　　　And their judicial, legislative and
　　　　　　　Administrative bodies are now merged.

Europa:　　　　The European Union has begun.

(Lights dim and then brighten. 1 January 1973. Film shows the UK, Ireland and Denmark joining the EC. The REPRESENTATIVES OF THE UK, IRELAND AND DENMARK *step forward and chant. Film on screen of 1973 enlargement.)*

UK, Ireland
and Denmark:　　The UK, Ireland and Denmark have joined
　　　　　　　To give the EC its first enlargement.

(Lights dim and then brighten. 1 January 1981. Monnet has put on a black cloak and has joined the shades on the left of the stage. Film on screen shows Greece joining the EC. The REPRESENTATIVE OF GREECE steps forward and chants.)

Greece: And now Greece has joined the growing EC
           In its second dynamic enlargement.

(The WISE MEN confer with Europa. From now on the Twelve Wise Men, the original nine and three recently deceased VIPs, chant as a chorus. A name in square brackets, as in the case of Kant below, indicates that a subject is within the specialist expertise of one particular Wise Man, and this specialist may be given one or more of the Wise Men's lines, as the director sees fit.)

Wise Men: You will need to abolish all borders.
[Kant]

(Lights dim and then brighten. 14 June 1985. Schengen, Luxembourg. Film on screen shows the signing of the Schengen Agreement in the town of Schengen in Luxembourg, by five of the ten member states of the EEC: the three states of the Benelux Economic Union, West Germany and France. The FIVE REPRESENTA- TIVES speak.)

The five: We have all just agreed to the gradual
            Abolition of border checks and in
            Ten years' time we'll live in a single state
            With no internal border restrictions.

Europa: My dream is nearer. One day there will be
            Twenty-six borderless European states.

(Lights dim and then brighten. 1 January 1986. Film on screen shows Spain and Portugal joining the EC. The REPRESENTATIVES OF SPAIN AND PORTUGAL *step forward and chant.)*

Spain and
Portugal:

And now both Spain and Portugal have joined
In the growing EC's third enlargement.
But Greenland, granted home rule by Denmark,
Has voted to withdraw from the EC.

(The WISE MEN *step forward and confer with* EUROPA.)

Wise Men:
[Ficino, Schuman]

You need a single market urgently
And political co-operation.

Europa:

Our Single European Act's the first
Revision of the first Treaty of Rome.
It will create a single market in
The European Community by
Nineteen ninety-two and commence my dream.
Nine countries have signed this Act, step forward.

(Each of the NINE REPRESENTATIVES *names his or her country.)*

Chorus of nine:

We have all signed. Belgium. West Germany.
France. Ireland. Luxembourg. The Netherlands.
Portugal. Spain. The United Kingdom.

(Lights dim and then brighten. 17 February 1986. Luxembourg. Film on screen shows the Single European Act, which revises the Treaties of Rome, being signed in Luxembourg by nine member states: Belgium, West Germany, France, Ireland, Luxembourg, Netherlands,

Portugal, Spain and the UK. The NINE *step forward and chant.*)

The nine:
And now the Single European Act
That reforms institutions, extends powers,
Foreign policy co-operation
And the single market, and revises
The Treaties of Rome and adds momentum
To new European integration.

(*Lights dim and then brighten. 28 February 1986. Film on screen shows Denmark, Italy and Greece signing the Single European Act. Their* THREE REPRESENTA-TIVES *step forward and chant.*)

Denmark, Italy and Greece:
Denmark, Italy and Greece have now signed
The Single European Act to found
A single market within the EU.

(*Lights dim and then brighten. 9 November 1989. Film on screen of the Berlin Wall being breached. A* CHORUS OF 50 *chants.*)

Chorus of 50:
The Berlin Wall is breached after nearly
Three decades of keeping East Berliners
Apart from West Berliners. Germany
Can reunite and again dominate.

Europa:
The Berlin Wall has fallen, the Cold War
Is coming to an end. Soviet influence
Over Communist Europe will collapse.
Communist states will become free-market
Democracies, and we must be prepared
To enlarge Europe to include the East.

Wise Men: We are seeing in our exciting time
[Dante, Churchill] The reunification of Europe.

Europa: Yes, a resurgence will revitalise
And regenerate young Europeans.

Wise Men: History is like a winding spiral stair.
[More, Churchill] Nations ascend and find themselves above
Where they were placed not long previously,
And this time have a chance to get things right.

(*All the East-European and ex-Soviet representatives, a*
CHORUS OF THE EAST, *step forward and chant.*)

Chorus of the
East: We have endured hard times as Communists.
Now we can see a bright future ahead.

(*The* WISE MEN *step forward and confer with*
EUROPA.)

Wise Men: You need to create a European
[Augustus]   Union with its own single currency.

Europa: We will achieve that and we must strengthen
Europe's supranational institutions:
Our Commission, our Parliament and Court.

(*Lights dim and then brighten. 3 October 1990. Berlin.*
Film on screen shows the unification of Germany. The
representative of GERMANY *steps forward and*
speaks.)

Germany: Unification day, West Germany
Has absorbed East Germany, the German
Democratic Republic's ceased to exist.

Treaties West Germany signed continue.
The Berlin Wall came down and Germany –
First unified in 1871,
Merged with Saarland in 1957 –
Is now *re*united. I am so pleased.

Europa: One Germany acts out part of my dream.

(*Lights dim and then brighten. 7 February 1992.
Maastricht, Netherlands, inside the government
buildings of the Limburg province on the Maas. Film on
screen shows the signing of the Maastricht Treaty, the
Treaty on European Union. The twelve signatories are:
Belgium, Denmark, France, Germany, Greece, Ireland,
Italy, Luxembourg, Netherlands, Portugal, Spain and
the UK. Their representatives step forward and chant in
a* CHORUS OF 12.)

Chorus of 12:   We have signed the Treaty of Maastricht
Which renames the EEC and EC.
We've created the European Union
And a single European currency,
The euro, which will bond our free market.

Europa: We now have a supranational pillar
With two intergovernmental pillars
For committees drawn from our member states,
Foreign policy, military strength,
Criminal justice and judicial links –
All are now supranational, as should be.
We have control over inflation, debt,
Deficits and exchange and interest rates.
Our eurozone is now spectacular.

Wise Men: But you must prepare for more enlargement.
[Charlemagne]

(1 January 1995. Film on screen shows a new enlargement. The REPRESENTATIVES OF AUSTRIA, SWEDEN AND FINLAND *step forward and chant.)*

Austria, Sweden
and Finland:　Now Austria, Sweden and Finland have joined
The rich EU in its fourth enlargement.

Europa:　I wanted Norway but its government's
Lost a second national referendum.

(Lights dim and then brighten. 26 March 1995. Film on screen shows the implementation of the Schengen Agreement and establishment of the Schengen Area. EUROPA *speaks.)*

Europa:　The Schengen Area's now implemented.
The signatories have a single state
And have no internal border control.

(Lights dim and then brighten. 2 October 1997. Amsterdam. Film on screen shows the signing of the Treaty of Amsterdam by 15 members of the EU: Belgium, Denmark, Finland, France, Greece, Ireland, Italy, Luxembourg, Netherlands, Portugal, Spain, the UK, Sweden, Germany and Austria. REPRESENTA-TIVES OF THE 15 *countries step forward and chant.)*

Chorus of 15:　The Treaty of Amsterdam focuses
On citizenship, rights, democracy
And employment, and brings Community
Freedom, security and justice to
Our common foreign and security
Policy. And the Schengen Area
Is now absorbed into the EU, which

Comprises a borderless single state
For all EU states except the UK
And Ireland, who have sadly opted out.

Wise Men:
[Napoleon,
Schuman]

You must reform the institutional
Structure of the European Union
To prepare for your eastward expansion.

(*Lights dim and then brighten. 7 December 2000. Film on screen showing the Charter of Fundamental Rights being proclaimed at the European Council, Nice, which comprises the heads of state or government of the EU member states, and being signed simultaneously by the Presidents of: the European Commission; the Council of the European Union, or Council of Ministers, which represents the executive governments of the EU's member states; and the European Parliament, which represents the legislature. A statement by the European Council through the President of the European Parliament, NICOLE FONTAINE.*)

Nicole Fontaine:

The European Council welcomes the joint
Proclamation by the European
Parliament, the Council of Ministers
And the Commission of the new Charter
Of Fundamental Rights, which combines in
A single text civil, political,
Economic, social and societal
Rights hitherto laid down in a number
Of international, European or
National sources. The European Council
Would like to see it disseminated
Widely among the Union's citizens.

(*All* 50 REPRESENTATIVES *chant as a chorus.*)

Chorus of 50:   Gone are the years of repression and fear,
                 Of Stalin and Hitler, of enslavement,
                 And now we Europeans rejoice in
                 Our new freedoms and our utopia
                 And the highest form of society
                 Humankind has yet known, which towers above
                 The societies of the past, now gone.
                 Our rights, freedoms and principles are found
                 In the gleaming words in the articles
                 Of the Charter of Fundamental Rights.

Europa: Let's hear the articles of the Charter.

Chorus of 50:   Listen to simple words with huge meanings.

                 (*Each of the* 50 REPRESENTATIVES *recites an article
                 of the Charter of Fundamental Rights of the Union.
                 Each article is grouped under a title or heading, and on
                 screen is the title, 'Dignity', followed by its articles. See
                 Appendix 3. Each title is introduced by one of the Wise
                 Men.* FICINO *speaks.*)

Ficino: Citizens' dignity is protected.

Germany: Human dignity's inviolable.
                 It must be respected and protected.

Italy: Everyone has the right to life, free from
                 The death penalty and execution.

UK: Physical and mental integrity
                 Must be respected in everybody.

Ireland: No one shall be subjected to torture
                 Or inhuman, degrading punishment.

France: No one shall be held in slavery or
Shall be required to perform forced labour.

(*The screen says 'Freedom' and more articles appear.*
AUGUSTUS *speaks.*)

Augustus: Citizens' freedom is now guaranteed.

Belgium: Everyone has the right to liberty
And the security of their person.

Netherlands: Everyone has the right to respect for
His or her private and family life.

Luxembourg: Everyone has the right to have personal
Data protected and to access it.

Austria: Everyone has the right to be married
And the right to found a new family.

Slovenia: Freedom of thought, conscience and religion
And conscientious objection are rights.

Malta: Freedom of expression and the media,
And to receive information, are rights.

Portugal: Freedom of peaceful assembly, of trade
Unions and association are rights.

Spain: The freedom of the arts and sciences
And all academic freedom are rights.

Cyprus: Free education for all and founding
Educational establishments are rights.

Croatia: Freedom to choose any occupation

And work in any Member State are rights.

Estonia: Everyone has the freedom to conduct
                  A business in accord with Union law.

Latvia: Everyone has the right to own and use
                  Acquired and intellectual property.

Lithuania: The right to asylum is guaranteed
                  By the Geneva Convention's firm rules.

Poland: No one may be removed to a State where
                  The death penalty or torture menace.

                  (*The screen says 'Equality' and more articles appear.*
                  NAPOLEON *speaks.*)

Napoleon: Citizens' equality is assured.

Hungary: Everyone is equal before the law.
                  No one at all can be above the law.

Czech Republic: There shall be no discrimination on
                  Grounds of sex, race, colour or origin.

Slovakia: There shall be no discrimination on
                  Grounds of language, religion or belief.

Bulgaria: There shall be no discrimination on
                  Grounds of national minority or birth.

Romania: There shall be no discrimination on
                  Grounds of disability, age or sex.

Greece: There shall be no discrimination on
                  Grounds of property or nationality.

Turkey: The Union shall respect diversity
              Of cultures, religions and languages.

Sweden: There must be equality between men
              And women in employment, work and pay.

Denmark: Children shall have the right to protection
              And care, and to express their views freely.

Finland: Every child has the right to have contact
              With both parents, and to its best interests.

Switzerland: The elderly have the right to a life
              Of dignity and to independence.

Iceland: The elderly have the right to take part
              In active social and cultural life.

Norway: The disabled must independently
              Take part in work and the community.

(*The screen says 'Solidarity' and more articles appear.*
CHARLEMAGNE *speaks.*)

Charlemagne: Citizens' solidarity is strong.

Liechtenstein: Workers have the right to information
               And consultation regarding their work.

Monaco: Workers and employers have the right of
              Collective bargaining and strike action.

Andorra: Everyone has the right of access to
              A free placement service for recruitment.

San Marino: All workers have the right to protection

Against their unjustified dismissal.

Serbia: All workers have the right to fair working
                   Conditions that respect health and safety.

Albania: All workers have the right to a limit
                   On working hours, rest periods and paid leave.

Kosovo: Child labour is prohibited, and young
                   People at work shall not be exploited.

Bosnia and
Herzegovina: The family shall enjoy the State's legal,
                   Economic and social protection.

Macedonia: All have the right to paid maternity
                   Leave and parental leave after a birth.

Montenegro: Social security and assistance
                   Covers illness, industrial accidents,

Moldova: Dependency, old age and loss of work,
                   And social and housing deprivation.

Ukraine: All have the right of access to health care
                   And preventative medical treatment.

Azerbaijan: All have the right to access services
                   That advance their economic interests.

Georgia: All have the right of environmental
                   Protection and improved environments.

Armenia: All consumers have the right to a high
                   Level of protection in consumption.

(The screen says 'Citizens' rights' and more articles appear. KANT speaks.)

Kant: Citizens' rights have all been safeguarded.

Russia: All have the right to vote in elections,
And stand in a free and secret ballot.

Belarus: And to vote and stand at municipal
Elections in the state where they reside.

Kazakhstan: And the right to good administration
That's impartial, with access to all files.

(All 50 REPRESENTATIVES chant as a chorus.)

Chorus of 50: Institutions must make good all damage
And grant access to all their documents.
Everyone has the right to petition
The European Parliament if pressed.
Every citizen has the right to move
And reside freely in the member states
As have nationals of third countries who live
In the territory of a member state.
All have the right to diplomatic and
Consular protection in third countries.

(The screen says 'Justice' and more articles appear. JUSTINIAN speaks.)

Justinian: Citizens' justice is now perfected.

Chorus of 50: Everyone whose rights are violated
Has the right to an effective remedy,
A fair hearing before a tribunal
Within a reasonable time and to be

Defended and apply for legal aid.
Everyone shall be presumed innocent
Until proved guilty according to law.
The rights of their defence are guaranteed.
No one shall be held guilty of a crime
If it was not a criminal offence
At the time when it was first committed.
The severity of penalties must
Not be disproportionate to the offence.
No one shall be retried for an offence
That's already been tried under the law.

*(The articles disappear from the screen. Film of the
signing of the Charter of Fundamental Rights of the
Union. The* 50 REPRESENTATIVES *chant as a chorus.)*

Chorus of 50:   Our United Europe's a paradise,
An ever closer union, a future
Based on peace and universal values
Held in common, of human dignity,
Freedom, equality, solidari-
-ty, democracy and the rule of law.
We live in freedom, in security
And justice and cultural diversity,
In freedom of speech and free expression,
In free movement of persons, services,
Goods and capital at national, local
And regional levels, and we all have
Freedom of establishment. Paradise.
No one who has studied our great Charter
Of Fundamental Rights of the Union
Can fail to be impressed by our free life
And the rights and principles we enjoy.

(The 12 WISE MEN *speak as a chorus.)*

12 Wise Men: [Augustus, Schuman]	This is all excellent, but, Europa, Europe must now turn into a new State With its own legal personality. It must be above all the nation-states, A federal State above the local states. It must have a President and its own Foreign Minister who can represent Europe's foreign policy to the world.

(*Lights dim and then brighten. 26 February 2001. Nice. Film on screen of the signing of the Treaty of Nice by 15 signatories: Belgium, Denmark, Finland, France, Greece, Ireland, Italy, Luxembourg, Netherlands, Portugal, Spain, the UK, Sweden, Germany and Austria. Their* CHORUS OF 15 *steps forward and chants.*)

Chorus of 15:	We've improved our governing procedures And our decision-making, and are now Ready for enlargement. We can absorb The former oppressed Eastern-*bloc* countries.
Europa:	Some say it's a technocratic treaty But I see it as opening Europe.

(*Lights dim and then brighten. 1 May 2004. 10* REPRE-SENTATIVES *step forward, those of Cyprus, the Czech Republic, Estonia, Hungary, Latvia, Lithuania, Malta, Poland, Slovakia and Slovenia. They chant and identify themselves, each representative calling the name of his or her country.*)

Chorus of 10:	We are the simultaneous accessions In the growing EU's fifth enlargement: Cyprus. The Czech Republic. Estonia. Hungary. Latvia, Lithuania.

Malta. Poland. Slovakia. Slovenia.

(Lights dim and brighten. 29 October 2004, Rome. Film on screen of 25 member states – the 15 of 26 February 2001 and the most recent 10 of 1 May 2004 – signing a Treaty establishing a Constitution for Europe. EUROPA speaks.)

Europa:　　　　The EU tried to replace past treaties
　　　　　　　With a single Treaty to establish
　　　　　　　A Constitution for Europe. Alas.
　　　　　　　Alas, the French and Dutch rejected it
　　　　　　　And brought ratification to an end.
　　　　　　　Nine Muses, please inspire the way forward.

(The NINE MUSES raise their arms and beam power into Europa. They point towards José Barroso.)

　　　　　　　Step forth José Barroso, President
　　　　　　　Of the European Commission. Please
　　　　　　　Advise me. What do you suggest we do?

(JOSÉ BARROSO emerges from the shadows and stands by Europa.)

José Barroso:　　We set up a group of Wise Men, sixteen
　　　　　　　Advisers from sixteen countries, chaired by
　　　　　　　An ex-Prime Minister of Italy,
　　　　　　　Giuliano Amato, who chaired our
　　　　　　　Report on enlargement. They will reflect
　　　　　　　For two or three years and issue a text
　　　　　　　Of a new EU treaty that includes
　　　　　　　Part Three of the EU Constitution
　　　　　　　The French and Dutch refused to ratify.

(Lights dim and brighten. 2 February 2007. Film on

screen of Bulgaria and Romania joining the EU.
EUROPA *speaks.*)

Europa: And now, Bulgaria and Romania
Are the latest to join our expansion
In the mighty EU's sixth enlargement.

(*Lights dim and brighten. 4 June 2007. Brussels. The*
Amato Group of Wise Men release the draft text of a
new EU Treaty at a press conference. GIULIANO
AMATO *speaks.*)

Giuliano Amato: For three years we've reflected and our group
Of Wise Men, the Amato Group, has now
Rewritten the Treaty establishing
A Constitution for Europe. We have
The draft text of a new EU treaty.
We have agreed to urge the Commission
To set up an Intergovernmental
Conference that would amend the Rome Treaty
On European Union, the Maastricht
Treaty establishing the European
Community and give to the Charter
Of Fundamental Rights a legally
Binding status. The new treaty would be
Based on the Constitution's first and fourth
Parts, and would amend all the past treaties
Rather than replace them with a new text.

Europa: Excellent. How will this new text be known?

(*Lights dim and brighten. 13 December 2007. The 15th-*
century Jerónimos Monastery, Lisbon. Film on screen
shows 27 members signing the Treaty of Lisbon. The 27
REPRESENTATIVES – *all the 28 members of the EU*
in 2015 except for Croatia – step forward and chant.)

representatives:	The text's become the Treaty of Lisbon.
	By our signatures we have amended
	All existing treaties and created
	A European Union that straddles
	A vast swathe of Europe and no less than
	Twenty-three different EU languages.

Wise Men:	We admire your achievement and give thanks,
[Erasmus,	And we congratulate you, Europa.
Churchill]	

(EUROPA *nods.*)

Europa:	The Council of Ministers' voting in
	Forty-five policy areas has changed.
	The European Parliament provides
	A great bicameral legislature
	Alongside the Council of Ministers
	And is now more powerful. The EU has
	Its own legal personality with
	A President of the European
	Council and a High Representative
	Of the Union for Foreign Affairs and
	Security Policy. And our bill
	Of rights, The Charter of Fundamental
	Rights, is now legally binding. Member
	States have a legal right and procedure
	To leave the EU. We have been most fair
	And are scrupulous towards member states.

(*Europa turns to the 27 representatives.*)

Rejoice and celebrate. Revels commence.

(*The 27 representatives dance with each other, gyrate in a circle until each has danced with all. The music is confident, majestic and unified. The dance is celebratory.)*

Revels

(Lights dim and brighten. 19 November 2009. The Council of Ministers' building in Brussels. A dinner to celebrate the 20th anniversary of the dismantling of the Berlin Wall, shortly before the Treaty of Lisbon comes into force on 1 December 2009. Film on screen of the 27 Heads of State or Government arriving. The 27 EU representatives step forward. BARROSO stands alongside Europa.)

Barroso: At a summit of twenty-seven Heads
Of State or Government over dinner
To select the first 'EU President'
And Foreign Minister with embassies,
The President of the European
Council and Prime Minister of Sweden,
Fredrik Reinfeldt, announced the final choice:
'EU President', Herman Van Rompuy,
Who now replaces him as President
Of the European Council; EU
Foreign Minister, Catherine Ashton.

Europa: My dream's fast becoming reality.
This is more cause for joy. Please celebrate.

(More celebratory music and dancing. Again the 27 representatives take part in a circle dance that involves all 27 REPRESENTATIVES circle dancing with each other.)

(While the dancing is taking place the WISE MEN approach Europa.)

Wise Men: We must have a benevolent outlook
[More, Monnet]   And rule like a constitutional monarch.
                 A banking crisis brings austerity.
                 Our Commission must not appear to be
                 An arrogant bureaucracy that's blind
                 To public opinion, like the worst kind
                 Of dictatorship, deaf to grievances.

Chorus of 27:   We have chosen the EU's President:
                 Herman Van Rompuy. We are delighted.
                 We know the banking crisis has slowed down
                 The economies in southern Europe
                 And created a eurozone crisis,
                 But compare our paradisal Europe,
                 Our rights and freedoms, our great principles,
                 With the Europe of our great-grandfathers.
                 There can be no doubt, Europe's been transformed
                 Over four generations from ruins
                 To a thriving, thrusting, unified State
                 That guarantees our Charter and our rights.
                 Europe is now free and democratic.

(*Lights dim and brighten. 1 December 2009, the day the
Treaty of Lisbon is implemented. Lisbon. BARROSO
faces the 27 representatives and addresses them.*)

Barroso: The Treaty of Lisbon's come into force
                 Today, and all Europe is rejoicing.
                 The Treaty of Lisbon puts citizens
                 At the heart of the European project.
                 We have a more democratic Europe
                 That is more transparent and efficient;
                 A Europe of rights and values, freedom,
                 Solidarity and security,
                 A Europe that will be an actor on
                 The global stage, a clear voice in the world.

Now we have a European President
And Foreign Minister with embassies.
And now let our joy explode in fireworks.

(*Sound of fireworks. All 50 representatives now dance the celebratory circle dance. The 50 representatives enter the audience and dance with the 'courtiers'. Europa bangs the floor with a free-standing lectern and beckons the 50 representatives back on stage. Uplifting, stirring orchestral music, Beethoven's 'Ode to Joy'. Ecstatic, celebratory dance.*)

Europa: Revelling's good, but our masque's not ended.
No more dancing with courtiers, back on stage.

(*The* WISE MEN *again approach Europa.*)

Wise Men: We see problems ahead, difficulties.
[Kant, Schuman] Be cautious regarding more enlargements.

(*Lights dim and brighten. 1 July 2013. The* CROATIAN REPRESENTATIVE *steps forward and speaks.*)

Croatia: And now Croatia has joined the EU
In its seventh enlargement, we are now
Twenty-eight member states, with more ahead.

(EUROPA *turns to the 50 representatives and extends both arms.*)

Europa: Excellent. Europe can include you all.

(*Lights dim and lighten. 1 November 2014, the day the new President of the European Commission, Jean-Claude Juncker, who has succeeded José Manuel*

Barroso, assumes office. Berlaymont building, Brussels.
Film on screen shows the first day of the new
Commission. EUROPA *stands with the new President*
of the European Commission, Jean-Claude Juncker,
before the large oval table on the 13th floor, and
addresses all 50 representatives.)

Europa:

Now the European Commission has
A new President in Jean-Claude Juncker,
Despite opposition from the UK,
And next month will see a new President
Of the European Council, Donald
Tusk, who will take over from Van Rompuy,
We should be cheering in a joyful time
Of forward-looking optimism, hope
And revelry. But I am not happy
With the way things are going in Europe.
I implement strategy, but all round
Europe I see tactics acting against
The direction I have set out, local
Irritants that have undermined my dream.
Step forth Angela Merkel, Chancellor
Of Germany, and now my adviser.
You are the central figure in Europe.
Please tell us how you see the way ahead.

(ANGELA MERKEL *appears from the shadows and*
stands beside EUROPA.)

Merkel:

The EU is in a time of challenge.
The southern European states question
Austerity and want youth employment,
More people-friendly, human policies:
Greece, Spain, France and Italy. Internal
Division and fragmentation have loomed.
Right- and left-wing populism has gained

In Denmark, France and Germany, and in
Sweden, Spain and Greece. Islam's a target
And protests can sometimes appear racist.
Rapid economic improvements will
Draw Europeans to the centre ground.
A return to consensus politics
Is much to be desired – stability
And sound money – but the banking crisis
And recession demoralised voters.
There are elections in Greece, Spain, Denmark,
The UK, Finland, Poland, Portugal
And Estonia. In the UK, UKIP,
The Greens and Scottish Nationalists usurp
The centre-left and centre-right parties,
And in Greece and Spain the centre is weak.
Elections are won on the centre ground.
And there are challenges of mass movements
Of peoples from newly admitted states
To states (like the UK) where they can have
More generous benefit than where they left.
Russian aggression dismembered Ukraine
By annexing Crimea, destabilised
Georgia and Moldova, Serbia, Bosnia,
Hungary and Slovakia as Putin seeks
To re-establish spheres of influence
Similar to those in the Soviet time.
Russia wants Europe to be as before
The Berlin Wall was breached and eastern states
Joined the EU as a defence against
Soviet disdain for their democracies.

Europa: What do you say to that, Jean-Claude Juncker?

(*President* JUNCKER *turns to* EUROPA.)

Juncker: I do agree that there is discontent.

I have reassured the Eurosceptics.
I have explained to them I do not want
A growing United States of Europe,
That I do not believe that Europe can
Be constructed against the nation-state.
But the sceptics have strongly-held beliefs
That, though erroneous, are still believed.
Some hold Europe's sinking from immigrants.

Merkel:

Huge protests against Islamisation
Have taken place in Germany and France
And other European countries, which
Protesters fear are being Islamised.
Their loud marches are like those that toppled
The Communist regime in East Berlin.

Europa:

You can address these issues. The inward-
Looking leaders of the UK and France
Can't make the weather and are reacting
To your self-assured juggling of events,
Multiple international challenges.
You have Europe's biggest economy.
The policy agenda's directed
From Berlin, not Brussels, Paris, London,
And you will dictate what happens to Greece.

Merkel:

Two hundred and forty billion euros
Have been loaned to Greece and are now at risk.
There is no appetite for more bail-outs.
I want to keep Greece in the eurozone
But do not want to grant more debt relief
As this may burden German taxpayers.
Greece may be sacrificed for the single
Currency's survival.

Europa:

But that is not

Likely. If Greece leaves, so may Italy,
Spain and Portugal, all anti-euro.
We'll make sure Greece stays in the eurozone.

Juncker: The sceptics sense the worst, want to believe
That the EU's a failed experiment,
That lights are going out in our Europe,
We will soon be in darkness, and order
Will be blotted out.

Merkel: But the eurozone
Is our order, and we must keep it going.

(EUROPA *addresses the 50 representatives.*)

Europa: The eurozone *must* be kept going, Greece
Must not be given a pretext to leave.
Europe *must* block Russia's expansionist
And anti-democratic intentions.
Europeans, we can't be complacent.
This is not the time for states to sever
Their links to our principles and treaties,
To question free movement or to withdraw
From the eurozone, change their currency.
We're prosperous and free but we must stick
Together, seek ever closer union
And unite against the Russian menace
And keep free movement and our principles.

(EUROPA *turns to Juncker.*)

You will take your oath of independence
And stick to free movement and principle.

(*Lights dim and brighten. 10 December 2014. The new
European Commission are swearing the oath of*

independence at the Court of Justice, Luxembourg. Film on screen of Jean-Claude Juncker, the new President of the European Commission, standing before a lectern and 28 judges of the College of Commissioners and 9 Advocates-General, totalling 37 judges in all, who are in red with white bibs and seated in a horseshoe. The 28 EU representatives have put on placards saying 'College of Commissioners', and they form themselves into a semicircle. Nine other representatives put on placards saying 'Advocates-General' and join them. With the remaining 13 representatives behind him, JUNCKER addresses the 37 judges and the audience.)

Juncker: Having been appointed the President
Of the European Commission by
The European Council, following
The vote of consent by the European
Parliament, I solemnly undertake
To respect the treaties and the Charter
Of Fundamental Rights of the Union
In the fulfilment of all my duties;
To be completely independent in
Carrying out my responsibilities
In the general interest of the Union;
In the performance of my tasks, neither
To seek nor take instructions from any
Government or other institution.
The oath we take today's a serious one,
An oath of independence and respect
For our Charter of Fundamental Rights,
A strong political commitment from
The whole College to ensure the Charter's
Respected and complied with in EU
Policies for which the Commission is
Responsible. It's no trifling matter:
We are nothing if not for our values.

(Lights dim and brighten. Afterwards. The 50 attentive representatives are talking among themselves. The WISE MEN approach EUROPA.)

Wise Men: The Charter of Fundamental Rights enshrines
[Augustus,   Freedom of movement, we see storms ahead.
Schuman]

(EUROPA turns to JUNCKER.)

Europa: You have sworn that you will pursue a course.

(JUNCKER joins EUROPA.)

Juncker: We have sworn our oath of independence
                 And to maintain our freedom of movement
                 Between the member states of our Union,
                 Despite all attempts to negotiate
                 A block on movement as immigration –

Europa: By the UK, which is in the EU
                 And in the EU Customs Union
                 And the European Economic
                 Area, but not in the Schengen Area
                 Or in the eurozone – half in, half out.
                 You have just sworn to uphold the Charter
                 Of Fundamental Rights and sworn before
                 Twenty-eight judges and nine Advocates-
                 General of the EU's Court of Justice.
                 You cannot compromise your solemn oath.
                 The UK must be rebuffed, and told No.

Juncker: We have no alternative, we'll stand firm.
                 The EU will reject without debate
                 Calls to change treaties in order to end
                 The free circulation of our workers.

(CHURCHILL *moves to* EUROPA's *side.*)

Churchill:

The UK saved Europe during the war.
We stood alone against the *Blitz* until
The Americans joined us for D-Day.
We liberated France and Benelux.
At Zurich I called for a United
States of Europe. You must bear this in mind.

Europa:

I honour your courage and leadership,
But the UK is taxing our patience.
It's obsessed with obstructing our advance.

(CHURCHILL *walks to the* UK REPRESENTATIVE
and addresses her.)

Churchill:

You're spoiling our revels. We here all want
A United States of Europe that ends
All war, famine, disease and poverty.
I'm glad we've had seventy years without war.
I've a message for your Prime Minister,
And more importantly for his right wing
And the narrow-minded UKIP leaders,
For all poor leadership and statesmanship.
Don't you remember the war? Don't you know
How terrible the state of Europe was
When the war ended? Now Europe's at peace.
War's impossible when economies
Are intertwined in trade and tourism
And territorial aggression's taboo.
We are witnessing the triumph of peace.
Stop spoiling this new world. I am ashamed
Of your narrow self-interest and concerns:
Immigrants, benefits being abused,
Crowded schools and hospitals, and money.
Where is the vision of unity I

Left behind, my legacy to my Age?

UK: Europe's moved on since your time, thank heavens.
                And the UK has moved on, and England.
                We have issues about our being swamped.
                Too many have poured into our country.

                (EUROPA *and* Juncker *advance to join* CHURCHILL
                and the UK.)

Europa: You, Britannia, have lost Churchill's vision.
                You flirt with isolationism, you
                Have forgotten that Europe's kept the peace
                First through an east-west balance of power
                And then through our great eastwards
                        enlargement.
                Where is the internationalism
                That built your Empire and ruled a quarter
                Of the world at the time of the Great War?
                Shame on you. I don't like their borrowing
                But part of me hopes the Socialists win
                The coming general election so that
                Your promised in-out referendum can
                Be cancelled, and renegotiation
                Indefinitely shelved. Churchill's vision
                Must return. Austerity has done well,
                The deficit left by your profligate
                So-called New Labour (that blames the banking
                Bail-outs for borrowing) has been reduced.
                But you have lost your sense of destiny
                And Opposition calls for your leaders.

Churchill: Labour has moved left, elections are won
                From the centre ground. Labour will not win.

(*The* UK REPRESENTATIVE *addresses* EUROPA *and Juncker.*)

UK: I've a message from our Prime Minister.
Your Commission has alienated us.
Your demands for an increased budget are
Unacceptable, and you've swamped our towns
With immigrants who clutter up our schools
And hospitals, and live off benefits.
It is simply a question of numbers,
Too many make use of your free movement.
You're arrogant and dictatorial.
You should rule like a constitutional
Monarch and protect our flooded regions,
Not abuse our warm-heartedness and take,
Take, take from our kind generosity.
You will have deserved it if we defect.
You'll only have yourselves to blame if we
Turn our backs on Europe and walk away
And join the Free Trade Area of Iceland,
Norway and Liechtenstein, and Switzerland.

Europa: Don't spoil the rejoicing with sour comments.

(*The Wise Men have joined Europa and Churchill. The* WISE MEN *speak confidentially to* EUROPA.)

Wise Men: We do not want the United Kingdom
[More, Monnet] To leave our Union, and we must not be
Intransigent, provocative or blind.
We must not ignore member states' feelings.

Europa: I agree. But leadership sets a course
That all are pleased to follow to receive
The benefits of common policies.
Certain principles – freedom of movement

In the Charter of Fundamental Rights
Is one – are sacrosanct and must be kept.
We need strong leadership and wise members.
Unwise leaders of member states will face
Elections at home and may be replaced.

(MERKEL *has joined Europa, Juncker and the Wise*
Men, and addresses the UK REPRESENTATIVE.)

Merkel:

Germany absorbs Muslim immigrants
Culturally while supporting its churches.
The UK sees them burdening public
Services, its health and education.
I've seen the Berlin Wall wall Europe in
From the East-German side, and I support
The EU as defender of freedom,
Democracy and liberalism in
All our states including Ukraine, which has
Had the Crimea usurped by Putin
And is facing the loss of East Ukraine.
I see myself as Chancellor of Europe
And I want the UK to stay within
The EU. I'll discuss how the UK
Can work within the European Union
But I'll support the party that will stay
Within our democratic, free EU.

(*The* UK REPRESENTATIVE *addresses* MERKEL *and*
Juncker.)

UK:

I've a message from our Prime Minister.
We want a cap on migrants but within
Existing EU laws. We too support
Freedom of movement, but not its abuse.
Migrants should have no unemployment pay
For six months, and should not send benefit

Back to their home countries for their children.
We'll cut millions of pounds of benefits
Picked up on arrival or sent abroad.
The EU should reform, UK stay in.

Merkel:

Any limits on migrants and access
To welfare must be within existing
EU laws. Payment of child benefit
Abroad is regulated and enshrined
In EU treaties, and all member states
Would have to alter them. Most do not want
To re-open the treaties. I'll listen
But I can't speak for all the member states.
Asylum seekers besiege the EU,
Half a million a year from Syria,
The Middle East and from Eritrea,
Somalia and parts of Africa.
I need the UK's help in solving this.
I want the UK within the EU.
I don't want the EU's market to shrink,
Its exports to cost more, budget to fall.
All this would happen if the UK left.
I want the UK's military power.
I want help with the Mediterranean
Anti-austerity parties in Greece
And Spain, and with the Front National in France,
And with Italy, which doubts the euro.
In the Greek election next year leftist
Radicals are all set to come to power
Who want me to write off half the Greek debt
(As in 1953 in London
Half Germany's war debts were written off
To make our *Wirtschaftswunder* possible).
And will Spain, Portugal and Italy
Also want to halve their own debt burdens?
Europe's fractious and may be unstable

And we must insist that all existing
Austerity agreements are honoured.
I want Greece to stay in the eurozone.
I don't want hostility to free trade.
Europe's slipped into deflation, falling
Prices have weakened investment and growth.
I must permit quantitative easing
Of one point one trillion euros in all.
Austerity must stay realistic.
I need help with these difficult choices
As the troika of the European
Central Bank, IMF and Commission
Act as Greece's paymasters and grapple
With its debt burden. I need UK help
To maintain our monetary caution
And the EU's budgetary restraint.

(*The UK representative nods and returns to her place
among the 50 representatives.* JUNCKER *speaks to*
EUROPA.)

Juncker: We have sworn our oath of independence.

Wise Men: And you have done well and must now defend
[Justinian,   What you have sworn before Europe's judges.
Schuman]

Juncker: There is no more enlargement for five years.

(EUROPA *speaks to both Juncker and the 50 represen-
tatives.*)

Europa: There should be thirty-six member states from
                  Twenty twenty, after accession talks.
                  Ahead, albeit in the next decade,
                  Is the mighty EU's eighth enlargement:

Albania, Iceland, Macedonia,
Montenegro, Serbia and Turkey are
All official candidates, and Bosnia
And Herzegovina and Kosovo
Are potential candidates. Moldova,
Ukraine and Georgia have aspirations
To join the EU. And we still await
Switzerland, who froze its application,
And Norway, who withdrew its admission
Three times. Three Dutch Caribbean islands
May enter the EU now they have been
Integrated into the Netherlands.
Europe's like a great tree with many roots
In the rich soil of the Roman Empire,
And fifty branches, one for each nation,
And leaves that show each nation's history,
And all are nourished by the sturdy trunk
That grew during the dark Middle Ages,
Our European civilization's
History tree, 'Geschichtsbaum Europa',
Our story-telling, unifying tree.

(*The tree of European civilization, 'Geschichtsbaum
Europa', has appeared on screen. see* pp.118–9.)

I have a dream, I see it so clearly,
Look, ahead, Europeans, all fifty
Of us (if we exclude the Vatican,
Which is a palace, not a microstate,
And Kyrgyzstan, which is too marginal)
Will one day be in the enlarged EU,
The same number of states as the US,
And among the fifty will be Russia
And (in Ukraine) our beloved Crimea.
That is my dream, which I will deliver:
A United States of Europe that has

Fifty states and will, through diplomacy,
Bring in a free, democratic World State
That will improve the lot of humankind.
Leaders who defy us will quietly fall,
Fade away when the people vote them out.
The UK will remain in the Union.
Today the new Commission's been sworn in,
Don't let disagreements spoil your delight.
Now is a time for rejoicing as we
Turn to our newly-sworn Commissioners
And revel in the joy our citizens –
The eight hundred and twenty million in
The Council of Europe's forty-seven states –
All feel and share at the coming good times.

(*General rejoicing. Music: Beethoven's 'Ode to Joy'
which is based on Schiller's poem, 'Ode to Joy', the
anthem of the Council of Europe and of the EU. The
European flag with 12 gold stars is raised. Alongside it
a new European flag containing 50 gold stars in a circle
is raised. The 50 representatives shake hands with and
hug each other. Then the* 28 EU REPRESENTATIVES
*step forward and put on large badges saying
'Commissioner'. The 28 Commissioners shake hands
with or embrace each other. The Muses play and sing.
Film on screen of unified Europeans after the oath of
independence. The 50 representatives return to their
positions in 17 supranational bodies. All the representa-
tives of the European supranational bodies now express
their joy in turn and chant their welcome to the new
Commission and the new Europe. Some representatives
belong to more than one body – indeed, some belong to
several bodies – and will speak several times.*)

28 EU
representatives: We twenty-eight EU member states praise

Our single market and system of laws,
Our free movement of people, services,
Goods and capital throughout our Europe
Among five hundred million citizens.
We're pleased with the way everything has gone.
We salute the oath of independence.

32 EU Customs
Union
representatives: We thirty-two EU Customs Union
States – including Turkey and microstates
Andorra, Monaco, San Marino –
Rejoice in taking part in the EU.
We have prospects and can live the good life.

19 eurozone
representatives: We nineteen eurozone states rejoice in
Our use of the euro in our market.
Two more – the UK, Denmark – have to meet
Criteria, four more have agreements
To use the euro as their currency
And issue euro coins. And Kosovo
And Montenegro, though outside the zone,
Use the euro unilaterally.
The financial crisis has weakened us
And left Greece tottering upon the brink
But we have regrouped and are prospering,
And we rejoice in our common tender.

26 Schengen Area
representatives: We twenty-six Schengen states –the EU
Except Bulgaria, Croatia, Cyprus,
Ireland, Romania, the UK, with four
EFTA states, Iceland, Norway, Liechtenstein
And Switzerland – have abolished passport
And border controls to ease free movement

Of goods, information, money, people.
We are pleased with all that has been achieved.

30 European
Economic Area
representatives:
We thirty states of the European
Economic Area – the EU (but
Not Croatia yet) and three EFTA states,
Iceland, Norway and Liechtenstein – have free
Movement of goods, persons, services and
Capital through our states and can admit
European Free Trade states to the EU's
Internal market though they aren't members.
We welcome the prospect of enlargement.

4 European Free
Trade Association
representatives:
We four European Free Trade *bloc* states –
Iceland, Norway, Liechtenstein, Switzerland –
Kept out of the EU by voters or
By choice, used to be ten but have dwindled.
We're all right as we are but still wonder
If we should really be in the EU.

7 Central
European Free
Trade
Agreement
representatives:
We seven Central European Free Trade
Agreement states – Albania, Bosnia
And Herzegovina, Macedonia,
Moldova, Montenegro, Serbia
And the UN mission in Kosovo –
Are preparing for EU membership
By operating our free trade area.
We are happy with new Commissioners.

4 GUAM
representatives:

We four GUAM states – that's Georgia and
    Ukraine,
Azerbaijan and Moldova – pursue
Integration with Europe, we promote
Democratic values in our borders
And our economic development.
We want to join the EU in due course.

12 Organisation
of the Black Sea
Economic
Co-operation
(BSEC)
representatives:

We twelve Organisation of the Black Sea
Economic Co-operation states
Work for stability in the Black Sea
Region and seek prosperity for all.
We warmly welcome new Commissioners.

2 Union State
representatives:

We, Russia and Belarus, have our own
Union State though Russia is in BSEC.
We take note of the new Commissioners.

*(Representatives from 6 other supranational bodies now
chant. They individually chant the names of their body.
For example, the representatives from Sweden,
Denmark, Finland chant 'The Nordic Council'.)*

Representatives
from 6 other
supranational
bodies:

The rest of the supranational bodies,
The Nordic Council and Visegrád Group,
The Baltic Assembly and Benelux,

The Common Travel Area, also
The Monetary Agreement with the EU,
All warmly welcome new Commissioners.

Europa: I long for when you'll all be member states.

47 Council of
Europe
representatives: We forty-seven Council of Europe states
Who promote legal standards, human rights,
Democratic development, the rule
Of law and cultural co-operation
Uphold essential European values
That were ignored in Nazi killing camps.
We rejoice in our stand for human rights
Among eight hundred and twenty million
Europeans, the backbone of Europe.

(5 REPRESENTATIVES *of the Eurasian Customs
Union, which is outside the EU, step forward: the repre-
sentatives of Armenia, Belarus, Kazakhstan,
Kyrgyzstan – not in the 17 EU supranational bodies
and here represented by Moldova wearing a placard
saying 'Kyrgyzstan' – and Russia.*)

5 Eurasian
Customs Union
representatives: We five Eurasian Customs Union states –
First Belarus, Kazakhstan and Russia,
Now also Armenia and Kyrgyzstan –
Are now an economic alliance
Of former Soviet Union states.
We have no connection with the EU,
We've removed internal borders and have
Revived the Soviet Union in our states
Despite opposition from the US

That sees us as Russian-dominated.
We don't care about the new Commission.

Europa: You need to integrate with the EU.
You really want to join, I know you do.

(*All the 50 representatives have now spoken within their 17 supranational bodies. Now all* 50 REPRESENTA-TIVES *chant as a chorus.*)

Chorus of all 50: Seventy years back Europe was in ruins.
Our lot was misery and wretchedness.
Now Europe has been transformed over four
Generations to a unified State.
We live in hope, we have prospects, we all
Have futures in our fifty post-war states.
Our Europe's interconnecting circles
Are like cog-wheels that engage other cogs
And transfer motion so the Union runs.

(EUROPA *addresses the 50 representatives.*)

Europa: Thank you, my fifty European states.
One day you will all be in the EU.
The day will come when you're all in Europe's
Most advanced state ever. My dream is now
That liberal democracy will be proved
The ideal government for the World State
That will transform the lives of humankind.

(*Uplifting, stirring music. Celebratory dance.*)

Epilogue

(EUROPA *turns to Zeus, who rises to his feet*
unsteadily.)

Europa:

Lord of all, who has worked tirelessly for
The peaceful harmony of humankind
And has sought to create a paradise
For undeserving man to inhabit,
I've set up an ideal State in Europe
That can now spread and be widely followed
Now that a structure has been created.
I have established your grandiose vision
Where it was most needed, in smashed Europe.
I present you with the utopia
You've wanted for our disunited earth.
On one of the five continents, at least,
Tyranny and dictatorship can now
Be seen to be ending for a World State
That's democratic, constitutional.
The hard work's done, further expansion will
Follow as a stream widens to the sea.
Nine Muses, twelve Wise Men, I discharge you.
We thank you for the Europe you've inspired.
Lord of all, I hope the EU's pleased you.
You may like to take back your utopia.

(ZEUS *steps forward, slightly doddery.*)

Zeus

(*to Europa*): You have done well, my goddess
      Europa.
Congratulations on implementing
My order and your supporting vision.
Europe will be a paradisal State.
But as you know, disorder is still rife

71

And that is just a start, there's much to do.
There has to be a unified North and
South America, Europe, Africa,
Middle East, West, Central and East Asia,
And then a unification of all
The continents into one free World State.
Your work has been a tiny part of all
The work that's needed to be done, but you
Have made a valuable contribution.
We will continue to work together
While you attract fifty states round your smile.
(*To all*): Know that the World State will abolish war,
Famine and disease, poverty and debt
By international law that will also
Bring in disarmament, solve energy
And environmental problems so there
Is the prospect of perpetual peace.
(*Aside*): The rise of a democratic World State
Will first challenge and then loosen the grip
Of the self-interested *élite* that seeks
To control the earth's resources – the oil
And gas, the banks and all the governments –
For its own ends and amass more trillions.
We have to work with the *élite* which funds
The banks and budgets, all expenditure,
But as soon as the structures they've financed
Are in place we will dump the Syndicate.
(*To all*): In all parts of the globe I want to see
Unions of states and policies that lead
To humankind's reunification
Through Universalist, not nationalist,
Thinking, through a vision of unity.
A new Universalism shines through
The Charter's universal articles.
(*To Europa*): I have the vision and the perspective,
I can see what must happen, but I'm tired

From urging a benevolent World State
On recalcitrant mankind, on people
Who don't listen, make mistakes, get things wrong,
Who're obstinately dim, disobedient.
Sometimes I think I've got too old for this,
It may be better to leave humankind
To their own self-destructive nation-states.
Thank you for taking from me the burden
Of removing some nation-states' borders
And getting Europe into Union.
(*To all*): The work has not finished, it's just begun.
The end of the beginning's not in sight.
But we can now see clearly what's ahead.
Now Europe has passed from occupation
And division to peaceful Union,
Enlargement and expansion, resurgence,
There's a new Renaissance that all can sense,
Not slow decline or collapse as some thought.
Despite some disquiet, Europe's transmuted,
It's been transformed by the triumph of peace.
It has prospects and plainly promises
Prosperity to a seventh of mankind.
Ahead's an Age of plenty and of peace.
Rise up and give an optimistic cheer
For all the problems can be overcome
And we are making progress in the world.
And ahead's a new Golden Age for all.

(*Dance, film and music blend in a memorable finale in
which the 50 representatives leave their supranational
bodies and groups, link hands and join into one united
circle.*)

19–24, 27–31 December 2014; 1–6, 10–18 January 2015

Timeline

The Growth and Enlargement of Europe

8 May 1945   Victory in Europe Day, formal end of the Second
                    World War

4 December 1945   Jean Monnet's proposals to modernise and
                    rebuild the French economy, the Monnet Plan,
                    submitted to General de Gaulle

14 July 1946   Winston Churchill calls for Franco-German
                    reconciliation in a united Europe in a speech in
                    Metz

19 September 1946   Churchill calls for the creation of a kind of
                    United States of Europe in a speech at Zurich
                    University

1 January 1948   The Customs Union between Belgium,
                    Netherlands and Luxembourg comes into force

17 March 1948   Signing of the Treaty of Brussels by Belgium,
                    France, Luxembourg, Netherlands and the UK

5 May 1949   Signing of the Treaty of London to establish the
                    Council of Europe

16 May 1949   Robert Schuman announces coming suprana-
                    tional Communities in the Festival Hall in
                    Strasbourg

23 September 1949   Schuman speaks at the fourth session of the
                    United Nations General Assembly

9 May 1950	Schuman presents The Schuman Declaration proposing a new European Coal and Steel Community in the Salon de l'Horloge of the Quai d'Orsay, Paris
18 April 1951	Signing of the Treaty of Paris in the Salon de l'Horloge of the Quai d'Orsay, Paris
3 September 1953	The European Convention on Human Rights comes into force
29 May 1954	The Bilderberg Group meets at Hotel De Bilderberg, Oosterbeek, Netherlands
23 October 1954	Paris Conference in which participating powers including Belgium, Canada, Denmark, France, Greece, Iceland, Italy, Luxembourg, Netherlands, Norway, Portugal, Turkey, the UK and the US reach agreement on West Germany
5 May 1955	Monnet resigns on Europe Day following the failure of the European Defence Community
9 July 1955 – 20 April 1956	The Intergovernmental Committee set up by the Messina Conference in Brussels meet
21 April 1956	Paul-Henri Spaak presents his Report on the General Common Market
26 June 1956	First day of the Intergovernmental Conference on the Common Market and Euratom
1 November 1956	Anglo-French invasion of Suez
4 November 1956	Soviet invasion of Hungary

25 March 1957	Signing of the Treaty of Rome at the Palazzo dei Conservatori on Capitoline Hill, Rome
4 September 1963	Death of Schuman
24 January 1965	Death of Churchill
8 April 1965	Signing of the Merger Treaty by Belgium, France, West Germany, Italy, Luxembourg and Netherlands
1 July 1967	The Merger Treaty comes into force
1 January 1973	First enlargement of the EC. The UK, Ireland and Denmark join
16 March 1979	Death of Monnet
1 January 1981	Second enlargement of the EC. Greece joins
14 June 1985	Signing of the Schengen Agreement by Belgium, Netherlands, Luxembourg, West Germany and France in Schengen, Luxembourg
1 January 1986	Third enlargement of the EC. Spain and Portugal join
17 February 1986	Signing of the Single European Act revising the Treaties of Rome by Belgium, West Germany, France, Ireland, Luxembourg, Netherlands, Portugal, Spain and the UK in Luxembourg
28 February 1986	Signing of the Single European Act by Denmark, Italy and Greece
9 November 1989	The Berlin Wall is breached

3 October 1990	Unification of Germany

7 February 1992   Signing of the Maastricht Treaty by Belgium, Denmark, France, Germany, Greece, Ireland, Italy, Luxembourg, Netherlands, Portugal, Spain and the UK

1 January 1995   Fourth enlargement of the EU. Austria, Sweden and Finland join

26 March 1995   Implementation of the Schengen Agreement

2 October 1997   Signing of the Treaty of Amsterdam by Belgium, Denmark, Finland, France, Greece, Ireland, Italy, Luxembourg, Netherlands, Portugal, Spain, the UK, Sweden, Germany and Austria

7 December 2000   The Charter of Fundamental Rights is proclaimed at the European Council, Nice and signed simultaneously by the Presidents of the European Commission; the Council of the European Union (or Council of Ministers, which represents the executive governments of the EU's member states); and the European Parliament (which represents the legislature). Statement by the European Council through the President of the European Parliament, Nicole Fontaine

26 February 2001   Signing of the Treaty of Nice by Belgium, Denmark, Finland, France, Greece, Ireland, Italy, Luxembourg, Netherlands, Portugal, Spain, the UK, Sweden, Germany and Austria

1 May 2004   Fifth enlargement of the EU. Cyprus, the Czech Republic, Estonia, Hungary, Latvia, Lithuania, Malta, Poland, Slovakia and Slovenia join

29 October 2004   Signing of a Treaty establishing a Constitution for Europe by 25 member states

2 February 2007   Sixth enlargement of the EU. Bulgaria and Romania join

4 June 2007   The Amato Group of Wise Men release the draft text of a new EU Treaty at a press conference in Brussels

13 December 2007   Signing of the Treaty of Lisbon by 27 members in the Jerónimos Monastery, Lisbon

19 November 2009   Dinner for 27 Heads of State or Government to celebrate the 20th anniversary of the dismantling of the Berlin Wall, Herman Van Rompuy declared 'EU President' (President of the European Council)

1 December 2009   The Treaty of Lisbon comes into force

1 July 2013   Seventh enlargement of the EU. Croatia joins

1 November 2014   The new President of the European Commission, Jean-Claude Juncker, who has succeeded José Manuel Barroso, assumes office in the Berlaymont building, Brussels

10 December 2014   The new European Commission swear the oath of independence at the Court of Justice, Luxembourg

APPENDIX

1

Groupings within Europe

(in alphabetical order)

1. 28 members of the EU in 2015:
    Austria, Belgium, Bulgaria, Croatia, Cyprus, Czech Republic,
    Denmark, Estonia, Finland, France, Germany, Greece, Hungary,
    Ireland, Italy, Latvia, Lithuania, Luxembourg, Malta,
    Netherlands, Poland, Portugal, Romania, Slovakia, Slovenia,
    Spain, Sweden, the UK

2. 22 states not yet members of the EU:
    Albania, Andorra, Armenia, Azerbaijan, Belarus, Bosnia and
    Herzegovina, Georgia, Iceland, Kazakhstan*, Kosovo,
    Liechtenstein, Macedonia, Moldova, Monaco, Montenegro,
    Norway, Russia, San Marino, Serbia, Switzerland, Turkey,
    Ukraine

    *EU–Kazakhstan bilateral agreement secures Kazakhstan's common
    foreign policy and trade relations with the EU.

3. 17 supranational bodies with the EU and members:

28 European Union (EU)	Austria, Belgium, Bulgaria, Croatia, Cyprus, Czech Republic, Denmark, Estonia, Finland, France, Germany, Greece, Hungary, Ireland, Italy, Latvia, Lithuania, Luxembourg, Malta, Netherlands, Poland, Portugal, Romania, Slovakia, Slovenia, Spain, Sweden, the UK

32 Customs Union

Andorra, Austria, Belgium, Bulgaria, Croatia, Cyprus, Czech Republic, Denmark, Estonia, Finland, France, Germany, Greece, Hungary, Ireland, Italy, Latvia, Lithuania, Luxembourg, Malta, Monaco, Netherlands, Poland, Portugal, Romania, San Marino, Slovakia, Slovenia, Spain, Sweden, Turkey, the UK

19 Eurozone

Austria, Belgium, Cyprus, Estonia, Finland, France, Germany, Greece, Ireland, Italy, Latvia, Lithuania, Luxembourg, Malta, Netherlands, Portugal, Slovakia, Slovenia, Spain

26* Schengen Area

Austria, Belgium, Czech Republic, Denmark, Estonia, Finland, France, Germany, Greece, Hungary, Iceland, Italy, Latvia, Liechtenstein, Lithuania, Luxembourg, Malta, Netherlands, Norway, Poland, Portugal, Slovakia, Slovenia, Spain, Sweden, Switzerland

*Bulgaria, Croatia, Cyprus and Romania are obliged to join the Schengen Area eventually, subject to assessment

30 European Economic
Area (EEA)

Austria, Belgium, Bulgaria,
Cyprus, Czech Republic,
Denmark, Estonia, Finland,
France, Germany, Greece,
Hungary, Iceland, Ireland,
Italy, Latvia, Liechtenstein,
Lithuania, Luxembourg, Malta,
Netherlands, Norway, Poland,
Portugal, Romania, Slovakia,
Slovenia, Spain, Sweden, the
UK

4 European Free Trade
Association (EFTA)

Iceland, Liechtenstein, Norway,
Switzerland

7 Central European Free Trade
Agreement (CEFTA)

Albania, Bosnia and
Herzegovina, Kosovo,
Macedonia, Moldova,
Montenegro, Serbia

4 GUAM

Azerbaijan, Georgia, Moldova,
Ukraine

12 Organisation of the Black Sea
Economic Co-operation (BSEC)

Albania, Armenia, Azerbaijan,
Bulgaria, Georgia, Greece,
Moldova, Romania, Russia,
Serbia, Turkey, Ukraine

2 Union State

Belarus, Russia

5 Nordic Council

Denmark, Finland, Iceland,
Norway, Sweden

4 Viségrad Group	Czech Republic, Hungary, Poland, Slovakia
3 Baltic Assembly	Estonia, Latvia, Lithuania
3 Benelux	Belgium, Luxembourg, Netherlands
2 Common Travel Area	Ireland, the UK
4 Monetary Agreement with the EU	Andorra, Monaco, San Marino, Vatican City
47 Council of Europe*	Belgium, Denmark, France, Ireland, Italy, Luxembourg, Netherlands, Norway, Sweden, the UK, Greece, Turkey, Iceland, Germany, Austria, Cyprus, Switzerland, Malta, Portugal, Spain, Liechtenstein, San Marino, Finland, Hungary, Poland, Bulgaria, Estonia, Lithuania, Slovenia, Czech Republic, Slovakia, Romania, Andorra, Latvia, Albania, Moldova, Macedonia, Ukraine, Russia, Croatia, Georgia, Armenia, Azerbaijan, Bosnia and Herzegovina, Serbia, Monaco, Montenegro

*in the order in which they joined

Outside EU:
5 Eurasian Customs Union	Armenia, Belarus, Kazakhstan,

Kyrgyzstan, Russia

4. 7 enlargements of the EC/EU:
(EC before 1993, EU after 1993)

| 1.1.1973 | 1st enlargement (3) |
| | Denmark, Ireland, the UK |

| 1.1.1981 | 2nd enlargement (1) |
| | Greece |

| 1.1.1986 | 3rd enlargement (2) |
| | Portugal, Spain |

| 1.1.1995 | 4th enlargement (3) |
| | Austria, Finland, Sweden |

| 1.5.2004 | 5th enlargement (10) |
| | Cyprus, Czech Republic, Estonia, Hungary, Latvia, Lithuania, Malta, Poland, Slovakia, Slovenia |

| 2.2.2007 | 6th enlargement (2) |
| | Bulgaria, Romania |

| 1.7.2013 | 7th enlargement (1) |
| | Croatia |

5.   Identification of 50 European flags: (See diagram on p.xviii.)

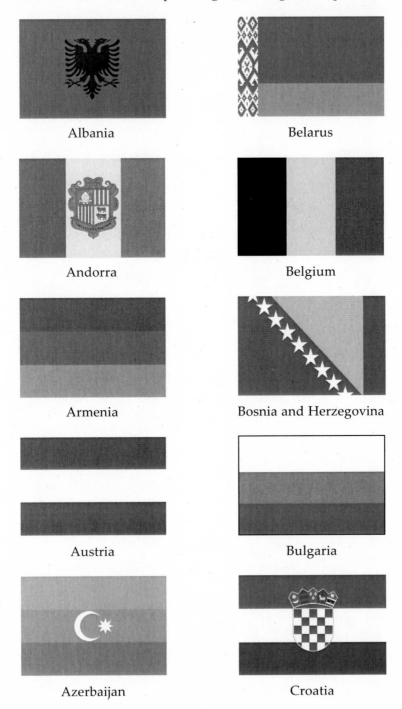

Albania	Belarus
Andorra	Belgium
Armenia	Bosnia and Herzegovina
Austria	Bulgaria
Azerbaijan	Croatia

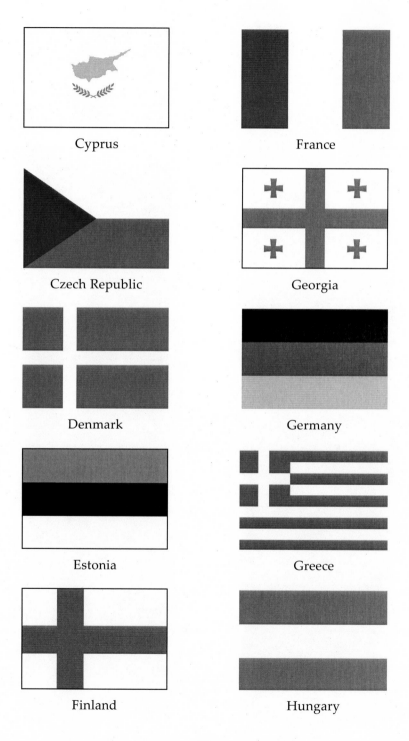

Cyprus

France

Czech Republic

Georgia

Denmark

Germany

Estonia

Greece

Finland

Hungary

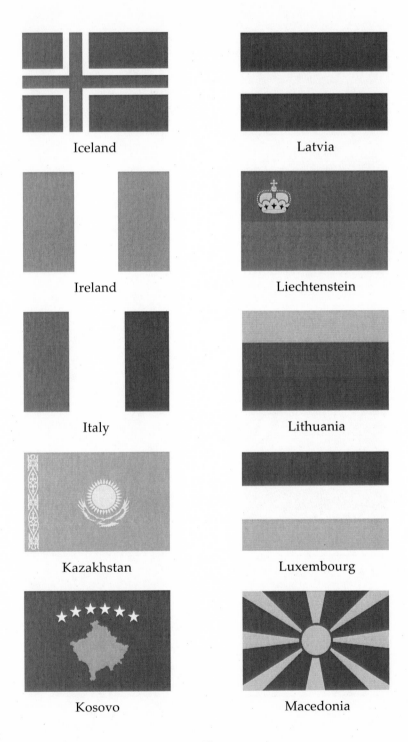

Iceland

Latvia

Ireland

Liechtenstein

Italy

Lithuania

Kazakhstan

Luxembourg

Kosovo

Macedonia

Malta

Norway

Moldova

Poland

Monaco

Portugal

Montenegro

Romania

Netherlands

Russia

San Marino

Sweden

Serbia

Switzerland

Slovakia

Turkey

Slovenia

Ukraine

Spain

United Kingdom

Vatican City*

*Vatican City too small to be regarded
as a European state

2

European Convention on Human Rights

Articles 1–19
1953

The Convention for the Protection of Human Rights and Fundamental Freedoms, better known as the European Convention on Human Rights, was signed in Rome by 12 member states of the Council of Europe (which Churchill had called to be set up) on 4 November 1950 and entered into force on 3 September 1953 (when Churchill was Prime Minister).

The Governments signatory hereto, being Members of the Council of Europe,

Considering the Universal Declaration of Human Rights proclaimed by the General Assembly of the United Nations on 10 December 1948;

Considering that this Declaration aims at securing the universal and effective recognition and observance of the Rights therein declared;

Considering that the aim of the Council of Europe is the achievement of greater unity between its Members and that one of the methods by which the aim is to be pursued is the maintenance and further realisation of Human Rights and Fundamental Freedoms;

Reaffirming their profound belief in those Fundamental Freedoms which are the foundation of justice and peace in the world and are best maintained on the one hand by an effective political democracy and on the other by a common understanding and observance of the Human Rights upon which they depend;

Being resolved, as the Governments of European countries which are like-minded and have a common heritage of political traditions, ideals, freedom and the rule of law to take the first steps for the collective enforcement of certain of the Rights stated in the Universal Declaration, Have agreed as follows:

Article 1 – *Obligation to respect Human Rights*
The High Contracting Parties shall secure to everyone within their juris-diction the rights and freedoms defined in Section I of this Convention.

SECTION I
RIGHTS AND FREEDOMS

Article 2 – *Right to life*
1. Everyone's right to life shall be protected by law. No one shall be deprived of his life intentionally save in the execution of a sentence of a court following his conviction of a crime for which this penalty is provided by law.

2. Deprivation of life shall not be regarded as inflicted in contravention of this article when it results from the use of force which is no more than absolutely necessary:
   (a)   in defence of any person from unlawful violence;
   (b)   in order to effect a lawful arrest or to prevent escape of a person unlawfully detained;
   (c)   in action lawfully taken for the purpose of quelling a riot or insurrection.

Article 3 – *Prohibition of torture*
No one shall be subjected to torture or to inhuman or degrading treatment or punishment.

Article 4 – *Prohibition of slavery and forced labour*
1. No one shall be held in slavery or servitude.

2. No one shall be required to perform forced or compulsory labour.

3. For the purpose of this article the term 'forced or compulsory labour' shall not include:
   (a)   any work required to be done in the ordinary course of detention imposed according to the provisions of Article 5 of this Convention or during conditional release from such

detention;

(b)   any service of a military character or, in case of conscientious objectors in countries where they are recognized, service exacted instead of compulsory military service;

(c)   any service exacted in case of an emergency or calamity threatening the life or well-being of the community;

(d)   any work or service which forms part of normal civic obligations.

Article 5 – *Right to liberty and security*

1. Everyone has the right to liberty and security of person. No one shall be deprived of his liberty save in the following cases and in accordance with a procedure prescribed by law:

    (a)   the lawful detention of a person after conviction by a competent court;

    (b)   the lawful arrest or detention of a person for non-compliance with the lawful order of a court or in order to secure the fulfilment of any obligation prescribed by law;

    (c)   the lawful arrest or detention of a person effected for the purpose of bringing him before the competent legal authority on reasonable suspicion of having committed an offence or when it is reasonably considered necessary to prevent his committing an offence or fleeing after having done so;

    (d)   the detention of a minor by lawful order for the purpose of educational supervision or his lawful detention for the purpose of bringing him before the competent legal authority;

    (e)   the lawful detention of persons for the prevention of the spreading of infectious diseases, of persons of unsound mind, alcoholics or drug addicts or vagrants;

    (f)   the lawful arrest or detention of a person to prevent his effecting an unauthorized entry into the country or of a person against whom action is being taken with a view to deportation or extradition.

2. Everyone who is arrested shall be informed promptly, in a language which he understands, of the reasons for his arrest and of any

charge against him.

3. Everyone arrested or detained in accordance with the provisions of paragraph 1(c) of this article shall be brought promptly before a judge or other officer authorized by law to exercise judicial power and shall be entitled to trial within a reasonable time or to release pending trial. Release may be conditioned by guarantees to appear for trial.

4. Everyone who is deprived of his liberty by arrest or detention shall be entitled to take proceedings by which the lawfulness of his detention shall be decided speedily by a court and his release ordered if the detention is not lawful.

5. Everyone who has been the victim of arrest or detention in contravention of the provisions of this article shall have an enforceable right to compensation.

Article 6 – *Right to a fair trial*
1. In the determination of his civil rights and obligations or of any criminal charge against him, everyone is entitled to a fair and public hearing within a reasonable time by an independent and impartial tribunal established by law. Judgement shall be pronounced publicly but the press and public may be excluded from all or part of the trial in the interests of morals, public order or national security in a democratic society, where the interests of juveniles or the protection of the private life of the parties so require, or to the extent strictly necessary in the opinion of the court in special circumstances where publicity would prejudice the interests of justice.

2. Everyone charged with a criminal offence shall be presumed innocent until proved guilty according to law.

3. Everyone charged with a criminal offence has the following minimum rights:
   (a)   to be informed promptly, in a language which he understands

and in detail, of the nature and cause of the accusation against him;

(b) to have adequate time and the facilities for the preparation of his defence;

(c) to defend himself in person or through legal assistance of his own choosing or, if he has not sufficient means to pay for legal assistance, to be given it free when the interests of justice so require;

(d) to examine or have examined witnesses against him and to obtain the attendance and examination of witnesses on his behalf under the same conditions as witnesses against him;

(e) to have the free assistance of an interpreter if he cannot understand or speak the language used in court.

Article 7 – *No punishment without law*

1. No one shall be held guilty of any criminal offence on account of any act or omission which did not constitute a criminal offence under national or international law at the time when it was committed. Nor shall a heavier penalty be imposed than the one that was applicable at the time the criminal offence was committed.

2. This Article shall not prejudice the trial and punishment of any person for any act or omission which, at the time when it was committed, was criminal according to the general principles of law recognised by civilized nations.

Article 8 – *Right to respect for private and family life*

1. Everyone has the right to respect for his private and family life, his home and his correspondence.

2. There shall be no interference by a public authority with the exercise of this right except such as is in accordance with the law and is necessary in a democratic society in the interests of national security, public safety or the economic well-being of the country, for the prevention of disorder or crime, for the protection of health or morals, or for the protection of the rights and freedoms of others.

Article 9 – *Freedom of thought, conscience and religion*

1. Everyone has the right to freedom of thought, conscience and religion; this right includes freedom to change his religion or belief, and freedom, either alone or in community with others and in public or private, to manifest his religion or belief, in worship, teaching, practice and observance.

2. Freedom to manifest one's religion or beliefs shall be subject only to such limitations as are prescribed by law and are necessary in a democratic society in the interests of public safety, for the protection of public order, health or morals, or the protection of the rights and freedoms of others.

Article 10 – *Freedom of expression*

1. Everyone has the right to freedom of expression. This right shall include freedom to hold opinions and to receive and impart information and ideas without interference by public authority and regardless of frontiers. This article shall not prevent States from requiring the licensing of broadcasting, television or cinema enterprises.

2. The exercise of these freedoms, since it carries with it duties and responsibilities, may be subject to such formalities, conditions, restrictions or penalties as are prescribed by law and are necessary in a democratic society, in the interests of national security, territorial integrity or public safety, for the prevention of disorder or crime, for the protection of health or morals, for the protection of the reputation or the rights of others, for preventing the disclosure of information received in confidence, or for maintaining the authority and impartiality of the judiciary.

Article 11 – *Freedom of assembly and association*

1. Everyone has the right to freedom of peaceful assembly and to freedom of association with others, including the right to form and to join trade unions for the protection of his interests.

2. No restrictions shall be placed on the exercise of these rights other than such as are prescribed by law and are necessary in a democratic society in the interests of national security or public safety, for the prevention of disorder or crime, for the protection of health or morals or for the protection of the rights and freedoms of others. This Article shall not prevent the imposition of lawful restrictions on the exercise of these rights by members of the armed forces, of the police or of the administration of the State.

Article 12 – *Right to marry*
Men and women of marriageable age have the right to marry and to found a family, according to the national laws governing the exercise of this right.

Article 13 – *Right to an effective remedy*
Everyone whose rights and freedoms as set forth in this Convention are violated shall have an effective remedy before a national authority notwithstanding that the violation has been committed by persons acting in an official capacity.

Article 14 – *Prohibition of discrimination*
The enjoyment of the rights and freedoms set forth in this Convention shall be secured without discrimination on any ground such as sex, race, colour, language, religion, political or other opinion, national or social origin, association with a national minority, property, birth or other status.

Article 15 – *Derogation in time of emergency*
1. In time of war or other public emergency threatening the life of the nation any High Contracting Party may take measures derogating from its obligations under this Convention to the extent strictly required by the exigencies of the situation, provided that such measures are not inconsistent with its other obligations under inter-national law.

2. No derogation from Article 2, except in respect of deaths resulting

from lawful acts of war, or from Articles 3, 4 (paragraph 1) and 7 shall be made under this provision.

3. Any High Contracting Party availing itself of this right of derogation shall keep the Secretary General of the Council of Europe fully informed of the measures which it has taken and the reasons therefor. It shall also inform the Secretary General of the Council of Europe when such measures have ceased to operate and the provisions of the Convention are again being fully executed.

Article 16 – *Restrictions on political activity of aliens*
Nothing in Articles 10, 11, and 14 shall be regarded as preventing the High Contracting Parties from imposing restrictions on the political activity of aliens.

Article 17 – *Prohibition of abuse of rights*
Nothing in this Convention may be interpreted as implying for any State, group or person any right to engage in any activity or perform any act aimed at the destruction of any of the rights and freedoms set forth herein or at their limitation to a greater extent than is provided for in the Convention.

Article 18 – *Limitation on use of restrictions on rights*
The restrictions permitted under this Convention to the said rights and freedoms shall not be applied for any purpose other than those for which they have been prescribed.

SECTION II
EUROPEAN COURT OF HUMAN RIGHTS

Article 19 – *Establishment of the Court*
To ensure the observance of the engagements undertaken by the High Contracting Parties in the Convention and the Protocols thereto, there shall be set up a European Court of Human Rights, hereinafter referred to as "the Court". It shall function on a permanent basis.

3

The Charter of Fundamental Rights of the Union
2000, 2007

A comparison of the italicised Article headings with the italicised headings of Articles 1–19 in the European Convention on Human Rights (*see* p.95) will confirm that the Charter grew out of the Convention.

PREAMBLE

The peoples of Europe, in creating an ever closer union among them, are resolved to share a peaceful future based on common values.

Conscious of its spiritual and moral heritage, the Union is founded on the indivisible, universal values of human dignity, freedom, equality and solidarity; it is based on the principles of democracy and the rule of law. It places the individual at the heart of its activities, by establishing the citizenship of the Union and by creating an area of freedom, security and justice.

The Union contributes to the preservation and to the development of these common values while respecting the diversity of the cultures and traditions of the peoples of Europe as well as the national identities of the Member States and the organisation of their public authorities at national, regional and local levels; it seeks to promote balanced and sustainable development and ensures free movement of persons, services, goods and capital, and the freedom of establishment.

To this end, it is necessary to strengthen the protection of fundamental rights in the light of changes in society, social progress and scientific and technological developments by making those rights more visible in a Charter.

This Charter reaffirms, with due regard for the powers and tasks of the Union and the principle of subsidiarity, the rights as they result, in particular, from the constitutional traditions and international obligations common to the Member States, the European Convention for the

Protection of Human Rights and Fundamental Freedoms, the Social Charters adopted by the Union and by the Council of Europe and the case-law of the Court of Justice of the European Union and of the European Court of Human Rights. In this context the Charter will be interpreted by the courts of the Union and the Member States with due regard to the explanations prepared under the authority of the Praesidium of the Convention which drafted the Charter and updated under the responsibility of the Praesidium of the European Convention.

Enjoyment of these rights entails responsibilities and duties with regard to other persons, to the human community and to future generations.

The Union therefore recognises the rights, freedoms and principles set out hereafter.

TITLE I
DIGNITY

Article II-61 *Human dignity*
Human dignity is inviolable. It must be respected and protected.

Article II-62 *Right to life*
1. Everyone has the right to life.

2. No one shall be condemned to the death penalty, or executed.

Article II-63 *Right to the integrity of the person*
1. Everyone has the right to respect for his or her physical and mental integrity.

2. In the fields of medicine and biology, the following must be respected in particular:
   (a) the free and informed consent of the person concerned, according to the procedures laid down by law;
   (b) the prohibition of eugenic practices, in particular those aiming at the selection of persons;
   (c) the prohibition on making the human body and its parts as such

a source of financial gain;

(d) the prohibition of the reproductive cloning of human beings.

Article II-64 *Prohibition of torture and inhuman or degrading treatment or punishment*

No one shall be subjected to torture or to inhuman or degrading treatment or punishment.

Article II-65 *Prohibition of slavery and forced labour*

1. No one shall be held in slavery or servitude.

2. No one shall be required to perform forced or compulsory labour.

3. Trafficking in human beings is prohibited.

TITLE II
FREEDOMS

Article II-66 *Right to liberty and security*

Everyone has the right to liberty and security of person.

Article II-67 *Respect for private and family life*

Everyone has the right to respect for his or her private and family life, home and communications.

Article II-68 *Protection of personal data*

1. Everyone has the right to the protection of personal data concerning him or her.

2. Such data must be processed fairly for specified purposes and on the basis of the consent of the person concerned or some other legitimate basis laid down by law. Everyone has the right of access to data which has been collected concerning him or her, and the right to have it rectified.

3. Compliance with these rules shall be subject to control by an

independent authority.

Article II-69 *Right to marry and right to found a family*
The right to marry and the right to found a family shall be guaranteed in accordance with the national laws governing the exercise of these rights.

Article II-70 *Freedom of thought, conscience and religion*
1. Everyone has the right to freedom of thought, conscience and religion. This right includes freedom to change religion or belief and freedom, either alone or in community with others and in public or in private, to manifest religion or belief, in worship, teaching, practice and observance.

2. The right to conscientious objection is recognised, in accordance with the national laws governing the exercise of this right.

Article II-71 *Freedom of expression and information*
1. Everyone has the right to freedom of expression. This right shall include freedom to hold opinions and to receive and impart information and ideas without interference by public authority and regardless of frontiers.

2. The freedom and pluralism of the media shall be respected.

Article II-72 *Freedom of assembly and of association*
1. Everyone has the right to freedom of peaceful assembly and to freedom of association at all levels, in particular in political, trade union and civic matters, which implies the right of everyone to form and to join trade unions for the protection of his or her interests.

2. Political parties at Union level contribute to expressing the political will of the citizens of the Union.

Article II-73 *Freedom of the arts and sciences*
The arts and scientific research shall be free of constraint. Academic

freedom shall be respected.

Article II-74 *Right to education*

1. Everyone has the right to education and to have access to vocational and continuing training.

2. This right includes the possibility to receive free compulsory education.

3. The freedom to found educational establishments with due respect for democratic principles and the right of parents to ensure the education and teaching of their children in conformity with their religious, philosophical and pedagogical convictions shall be respected, in accordance with the national laws governing the exercise of such freedom and right.

Article II-75 *Freedom to choose an occupation and right to engage in work*

1. Everyone has the right to engage in work and to pursue a freely chosen or accepted occupation.

2. Every citizen of the Union has the freedom to seek employment, to work, to exercise the right of establishment and to provide services in any Member State.

3. Nationals of third countries who are authorised to work in the territories of the Member States are entitled to working conditions equivalent to those of citizens of the Union.

Article II-76 *Freedom to conduct a business*

The freedom to conduct a business in accordance with Union law and national laws and practices is recognised.

Article II-77 *Right to property*

1. Everyone has the right to own, use, dispose of and bequeath his or her lawfully acquired possessions. No one may be deprived of his or her possessions, except in the public interest and in the cases and

under the conditions provided for by law, subject to fair compensation being paid in good time for their loss. The use of property may be regulated by law insofar as is necessary for the general interest.

2. Intellectual property shall be protected.

Article II-78 *Right to asylum*
The right to asylum shall be guaranteed with due respect for the rules of the Geneva Convention of 28 July 1951 and the Protocol of 31 January 1967 relating to the status of refugees and in accordance with the Constitution.

Article II-79 *Protection in the event of removal, expulsion or extradition*
1. Collective expulsions are prohibited.

2. No one may be removed, expelled or extradited to a State where there is a serious risk that he or she would be subjected to the death penalty, torture or other inhuman or degrading treatment or punishment.

TITLE III
EQUALITY

Article II-80 *Equality before the law*
Everyone is equal before the law.

Article II-81 *Non-discrimination*
1. Any discrimination based on any ground such as sex, race, colour, ethnic or social origin, genetic features, language, religion or belief, political or any other opinion, membership of a national minority, property, birth, disability, age or sexual orientation shall be prohibited.

2. Within the scope of application of the Constitution and without prejudice to any of its specific provisions, any discrimination on

grounds of nationality shall be prohibited.

Article II-82 *Cultural, religious and linguistic diversity*
The Union shall respect cultural, religious and linguistic diversity.

Article II-83 *Equality between women and men*
Equality between women and men must be ensured in all areas, including employment, work and pay.

The principle of equality shall not prevent the maintenance or adoption of measures providing for specific advantages in favour of the under-represented sex.

Article II-84 *The rights of the child*
1. Children shall have the right to such protection and care as is necessary for their well-being. They may express their views freely. Such views shall be taken into consideration on matters which concern them in accordance with their age and maturity.

2. In all actions relating to children, whether taken by public authorities or private institutions, the child's best interests must be a primary consideration.

3. Every child shall have the right to maintain on a regular basis a personal relationship and direct contact with both his or her parents, unless that is contrary to his or her interests.

Article II-85 *The rights of the elderly*
The Union recognises and respects the rights of the elderly to lead a life of dignity and independence and to participate in social and cultural life.

Article II-86 *Integration of persons with disabilities*
The Union recognises and respects the right of persons with disabilities to benefit from measures designed to ensure their independence, social and occupational integration and participation in the life of the community.

TITLE IV
SOLIDARITY

Article II-87 *Workers' right to information and consultation within the undertaking*
Workers or their representatives must, at the appropriate levels, be guaranteed information and consultation in good time in the cases and under the conditions provided for by Union law and national laws and practices.

Article II-88 *Right of collective bargaining and action*
Workers and employers, or their respective organisations, have, in accordance with Union law and national laws and practices, the right to negotiate and conclude collective agreements at the appropriate levels and, in cases of conflicts of interest, to take collective action to defend their interests, including strike action.

Article II-89 *Right of access to placement services*
Everyone has the right of access to a free placement service.

Article II-90 *Protection in the event of unjustified dismissal*
Every worker has the right to protection against unjustified dismissal, in accordance with Union law and national laws and practices.

Article II-91 *Fair and just working conditions*
1. Every worker has the right to working conditions which respect his or her health, safety and dignity.

2. Every worker has the right to limitation of maximum working hours, to daily and weekly rest periods and to an annual period of paid leave.

Article II-92 *Prohibition of child labour and protection of young people at work*
The employment of children is prohibited. The minimum age of admission to employment may not be lower than the minimum school-

leaving age, without prejudice to such rules as may be more favourable to young people and except for limited derogations.

Young people admitted to work must have working conditions appropriate to their age and be protected against economic exploitation and any work likely to harm their safety, health or physical, mental, moral or social development or to interfere with their education.

Article II-93 *Family and professional life*
1. The family shall enjoy legal, economic and social protection.

2. To reconcile family and professional life, everyone shall have the right to protection from dismissal for a reason connected with maternity and the right to paid maternity leave and to parental leave following the birth or adoption of a child.

Article II-94 *Social security and social assistance*
1. The Union recognises and respects the entitlement to social security benefits and social services providing protection in cases such as maternity, illness, industrial accidents, dependency or old age, and in the case of loss of employment, in accordance with the rules laid down by Union law and national laws and practices.

2. Everyone residing and moving legally within the European Union is entitled to social security benefits and social advantages in accordance with Union law and national laws and practices.

3. In order to combat social exclusion and poverty, the Union recognises and respects the right to social and housing assistance so as to ensure a decent existence for all those who lack sufficient resources, in accordance with the rules laid down by Union law and national laws and practices.

Article II-95 *Health care*
Everyone has the right of access to preventive health care and the right to benefit from medical treatment under the conditions established by national laws and practices. A high level of human health protection

shall be ensured in the definition and implementation of all Union policies and activities.

Article II-96 *Access to services of general economic interest*
The Union recognises and respects access to services of general economic interest as provided for in national laws and practices, in accordance with the Constitution, in order to promote the social and territorial cohesion of the Union.

Article II-97 *Environmental protection*
A high level of environmental protection and the improvement of the quality of the environment must be integrated into the policies of the Union and ensured in accordance with the principle of sustainable development.

Article II-98 *Consumer protection*
Union policies shall ensure a high level of consumer protection.

TITLE V
CITIZENS' RIGHTS

Article II-99 *Right to vote and to stand as a candidate at elections to the European Parliament*
1. Every citizen of the Union has the right to vote and to stand as a candidate at elections to the European Parliament in the Member State in which he or she resides, under the same conditions as nationals of that State.

2. Members of the European Parliament shall be elected by direct universal suffrage in a free and secret ballot.

Article II-100 *Right to vote and to stand as a candidate at municipal elections*
Every citizen of the Union has the right to vote and to stand as a candidate at municipal elections in the Member State in which he or she resides under the same conditions as nationals of that State.

Article II-101 *Right to good administration*

1. Every person has the right to have his or her affairs handled impartially, fairly and within a reasonable time by the institutions, bodies, offices and agencies of the Union.

2. This right includes:
   (a) the right of every person to be heard, before any individual measure which would affect him or her adversely is taken;
   (b) the right of every person to have access to his or her file, while respecting the legitimate interests of confidentiality and of professional and business secrecy;
   (c) the obligation of the administration to give reasons for its decisions.

3. Every person has the right to have the Union make good any damage caused by its institutions or by its servants in the performance of their duties, in accordance with the general principles common to the laws of the Member States.

4. Every person may write to the institutions of the Union in one of the languages of the Constitution and must have an answer in the same language.

Article II-102 *Right of access to documents*

Any citizen of the Union, and any natural or legal person residing or having its registered office in a Member State, has a right of access to documents of the institutions, bodies, offices and agencies of the Union, whatever their medium.

Article II-103 *European Ombudsman*

Any citizen of the Union and any natural or legal person residing or having its registered office in a Member State has the right to refer to the European Ombudsman cases of maladministration in the activities of the institutions, bodies, offices or agencies of the Union, with the exception of the Court of Justice of the European Union acting in its judicial role.

Article II-104 *Right to petition*
Any citizen of the Union and any natural or legal person residing or having its registered office in a Member State has the right to petition the European Parliament.

Article II-105 *Freedom of movement and of residence*
1. Every citizen of the Union has the right to move and reside freely within the territory of the Member States.

2. Freedom of movement and residence may be granted, in accordance with the Constitution, to nationals of third countries legally resident in the territory of a Member State.

Article II-106 *Diplomatic and consular protection*
Every citizen of the Union shall, in the territory of a third country in which the Member State of which he or she is a national is not represented, be entitled to protection by the diplomatic or consular authorities of any Member State, on the same conditions as the nationals of that Member State.

TITLE VI
JUSTICE

Article II-107 *Right to an effective remedy and to a fair trial*
Everyone whose rights and freedoms guaranteed by the law of the Union are violated has the right to an effective remedy before a tribunal in compliance with the conditions laid down in this Article.

Everyone is entitled to a fair and public hearing within a reasonable time by an independent and impartial tribunal previously established by law. Everyone shall have the possibility of being advised, defended and represented.

Legal aid shall be made available to those who lack sufficient resources insofar as such aid is necessary to ensure effective access to justice.

Article II-108 *Presumption of innocence and right of defence*
1. Everyone who has been charged shall be presumed innocent until proved guilty according to law.

2. Respect for the rights of the defence of anyone who has been charged shall be guaranteed.

Article II-109 *Principles of legality and proportionality of criminal offences and penalties*
1. No one shall be held guilty of any criminal offence on account of any act or omission which did not constitute a criminal offence under national law or international law at the time when it was committed. Nor shall a heavier penalty be imposed than that which was applicable at the time the criminal offence was committed. If, subsequent to the commission of a criminal offence, the law provides for a lighter penalty, that penalty shall be applicable.

2. This Article shall not prejudice the trial and punishment of any person for any act or omission which, at the time when it was committed, was criminal according to the general principles recognised by the community of nations.

3. The severity of penalties must not be disproportionate to the criminal offence.

Article II-110 *Right not to be tried or punished twice in criminal proceedings for the same criminal offence*
No one shall be liable to be tried or punished again in criminal proceedings for an offence for which he or she has already been finally acquitted or convicted within the Union in accordance with the law.

TITLE VII
GENERAL PROVISIONS GOVERNING THE INTERPRETATION AND APPLICATION OF THE CHARTER

Article II-111 *Field of application*

1. The provisions of this Charter are addressed to the institutions, bodies, offices and agencies of the Union with due regard for the principle of subsidiarity and to the Member States only when they are implementing Union law. They shall therefore respect the rights, observe the principles and promote the application thereof in accordance with their respective powers and respecting the limits of the powers of the Union as conferred on it in the other Parts of the Constitution.

2. This Charter does not extend the field of application of Union law beyond the powers of the Union or establish any new power or task for the Union, or modify powers and tasks defined in the other Parts of the Constitution.

Article II-112 *Scope and interpretation of rights and principles*

1. Any limitation on the exercise of the rights and freedoms recognised by this Charter must be provided for by law and respect the essence of those rights and freedoms. Subject to the principle of proportionality, limitations may be made only if they are necessary and genuinely meet objectives of general interest recognised by the Union or the need to protect the rights and freedoms of others.

2. Rights recognised by this Charter for which provision is made in other Parts of the Constitution shall be exercised under the conditions and within the limits defined by these relevant Parts.

3. Insofar as this Charter contains rights which correspond to rights guaranteed by the Convention for the Protection of Human Rights and Fundamental Freedoms, the meaning and scope of those rights shall be the same as those laid down by the said Convention. This provision shall not prevent Union law providing more extensive

protection.

4. Insofar as this Charter recognises fundamental rights as they result from the constitutional traditions common to the Member States, those rights shall be interpreted in harmony with those traditions.

5. The provisions of this Charter which contain principles may be implemented by legislative and executive acts taken by institutions, bodies, offices and agencies of the Union, and by acts of Member States when they are implementing Union law, in the exercise of their respective powers. They shall be judicially cognisable only in the interpretation of such acts and in the ruling on their legality.

6. Full account shall be taken of national laws and practices as specified in this Charter.

7. The explanations drawn up as a way of providing guidance in the interpretation of the Charter of Fundamental Rights shall be given due regard by the courts of the Union and of the Member States.

Article II-113 *Level of protection*

Nothing in this Charter shall be interpreted as restricting or adversely affecting human rights and fundamental freedoms as recognised, in their respective fields of application, by Union law and international law and by international agreements to which the Union or all the Member States are party, including the European Convention for the Protection of Human Rights and Fundamental Freedoms, and by the Member States' constitutions.

Article II-114 *Prohibition of abuse of rights*

Nothing in this Charter shall be interpreted as implying any right to engage in any activity or to perform any act aimed at the destruction of any of the rights and freedoms recognised in this Charter or at their limitation to a greater extent than is provided for herein.

4

The Tree of European Civilization

Geschichtsbaum Europa

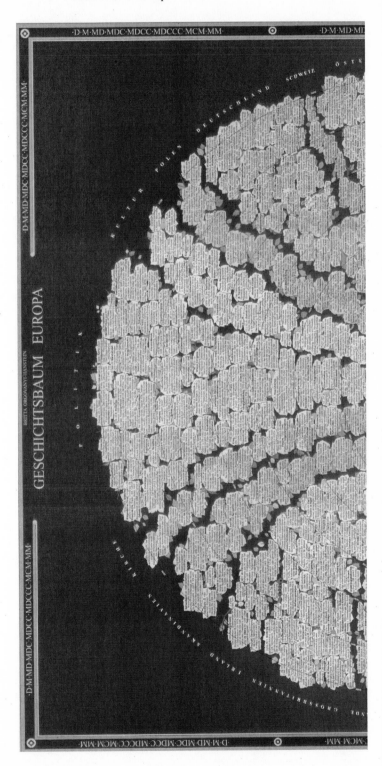

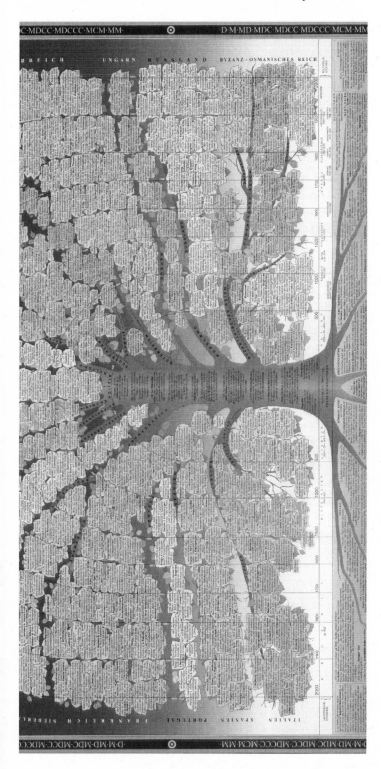

The tree of European civilizations, Geschichtsbaum Europa, with its eventual 50 branches (*see* p.64)

BOOKS

O is a symbol of the world, of oneness and unity; this eye represents knowledge and insight. We publish titles on general spirituality and living a spiritual life. We aim to inform and help you on your own journey in this life.

Visit our website: http://www.o-books.com

Find us on Facebook:
https://www.facebook.com/OBooks

Follow us on Twitter: @obooks